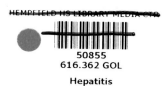
# Date Due

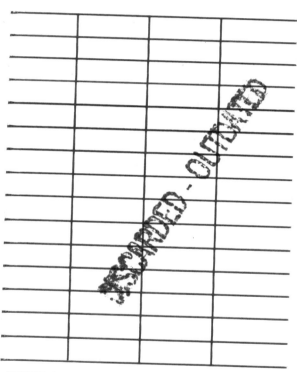

D1384367

# HEPATITIS

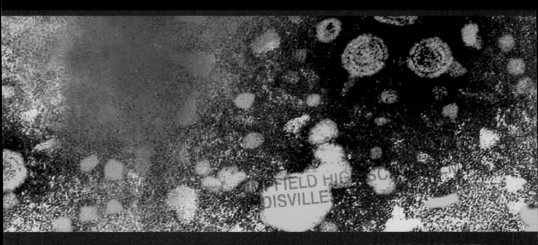

CONNIE GOLDSMITH

USA TODAY®, its logo, and associated graphics are federally registered trademarks. All rights are reserved. All USA TODAY text, graphics and photographs are used pursuant to a license and may not be reproduced, distributed or otherwise used without the express written consent of Gannett Co., Inc.

USA TODAY Snapshots®, graphics, and excerpts from USA TODAY articles on pages 6–7, 19, 20–21, 26–27, 36–37, 40–41, 49, 56–57, 64–65, 72, 76–77, 80, 89, 92, 98–99, 112–113, 116–117 © copyright 2011 by USA TODAY.

Twenty-First Century Books
A division of Lerner Publishing Group, Inc.
241 First Avenue North
Minneapolis, MN 55401 U.S.A.

Website address: www.lernerbooks.com

Library of Congress Cataloging-in-Publication Data

Goldsmith, Connie, 1945–
    Hepatitis / by Connie Goldsmith.
        p.   cm. — (USA TODAY health reports: diseases and disorders)
    Includes bibliographical references and index.
        ISBN 978–0–8225–6787–5 (lib. bdg. : alk. paper)
        1. Hepatitis—Juvenile literature.  I. Title.
    RC848.H42G65 2011
    616.3'623—dc22                                           2009020720

Manufactured in the United States of America
1 – DP – 7/15/10

# CONTENTS

**USA TODAY**
**HEALTH** REPORTS:
DISEASES AND DISORDERS

# THE NOBLE ORGAN

In ancient Greece, people would journey to an oracle, or fortune teller, to discover what the future held. The oracle would kill an animal, perhaps a goat or a sheep, to examine the creature's liver. A dark red liver that was smooth was a good sign. A pale liver that was bumpy foretold bad times ahead.

The liver has long been linked to human courage and strength. The earliest doctors thought that the liver was one of the three main organs of the body. The others were the heart and the brain. Around A.D. 200, the famous Roman doctor Galen declared the liver to be *the* most important human organ. He said (incorrectly) that it was the place where blood was formed. In 1653 English doctor William Harvey, whom historians credit with discovering how blood circulates, dubbed the liver the Noble Organ.

This nineteenth-century-style painting shows ancient Greeks consulting the Oracle of Delphi. Oracles would sometimes use livers to tell the future.

A healthy liver appears smooth and reddish brown.

Chances are you don't spend a lot of time thinking about your liver, even if it is a noble organ. And why should you? After all, when your liver is working properly, you can't hear it, see it, or feel it. You hear your stomach gurgling when it digests your breakfast. You see your chest moving when you breathe in and out. You feel your heart beating as it pumps blood through your body. Yet the liver is silent and hidden, invisible, tucked neatly away beneath your right rib cage. It is the biggest organ in the body and one of the busiest. An adult liver weighs only about 3.5 pounds (1.6 kilograms), but it performs about five hundred necessary tasks. Perhaps the most important is to filter poisonous toxins from the blood.

A lot of things can go wrong with the liver. For example, some people are born with abnormal livers. Others develop liver cancer or damage their livers by drinking too much alcohol. Sometimes livers are injured by drugs or accidents. Taking too much of the painkiller acetaminophen can damage the liver. And millions of people become infected each year by one of the several viruses that cause viral hepatitis. These viruses can severely damage the liver so that it no longer works properly.

www.usatoday.com

USA TODAY

Life

SECTION D

July 8, 2009

From the Pages of USA TODAY

# What is the bottom line on taking acetaminophen?

Last week, a Food and Drug Administration [FDA] committee gathered to discuss safety questions surrounding acetaminophen. They made several recommendations, such as lowering the maximum daily dosage, strengthening the labeling and removing the ingredient from some prescription drugs. The agency has not yet acted on the recommendations. USA TODAY medical reporter Mary Brophy Marcus asked a number of medical experts to weigh in on the news.

**Q: What prompted the meeting?**

A: Cases of acute liver failure and deaths related to acetaminophen have been increasing, says internist and pharmacist Judith Kramer, associate professor of medicine at Duke University Medical Center [in Pennsylvania].

**Q: Aside from Tylenol, what are some other medications that contain acetaminophen?**
A: The prescription medications Vicodin and Percocet as well as over-the-counter medications NyQuil, Excedrin and Tylenol cold and flu, says pharmacist Keith Veltri of Montefiore Medical Center in the

Three viruses, called the hepatitis A virus, hepatitis B virus, and hepatitis C virus, cause most cases of viral hepatitis. About thirty-two thousand Americans get hepatitis A each year. Hepatitis A is very common. About one-third of the U.S. population either has hepatitis A or has had it in the past. More than one million Americans have hepatitis B, and forty-six thousand are newly infected each year. Hepatitis C is the most common bloodborne disease in the United States. About 3.2 million Americans have hepatitis C. This makes hepatitis C (rather than acquired immunodeficiency syndrome, or AIDS) the most common bloodborne disease in the United States.

Bronx, N.Y. Many drugs that say "cold and flu" probably have acetaminophen for muscle pain and fever reduction, he says.

**Q: Is it true that hundreds of people die and tens of thousands more visit the hospital each year because of acetaminophen poisoning?**
A: Yes. An FDA memo reports an estimated 110,000 emergency room visits a year are related to acetaminophen, and several hundred cases of acute liver failure are also reported, Kramer says. Acetaminophen is the No. 1 reason people need liver transplants for acute liver failure, says Ronald Busuttil, chairman of surgery and chief of liver transplantation at UCLA Medical Center [in California].

**Q: Why is accidental overdose happening so often?**
A: Drug strength has increased, and labeling is not clear, Kramer says. Even more important, people are unaware that acetaminophen is in many medications, and they may reach a toxic dose without realizing it. You don't want to exceed 4,000 milligrams a day.

**Q: While we await FDA action, is it OK to keep using Tylenol, and how can patients avoid liver problems related to acetaminophen?**
A: Yes, it can be an effective, safe pain reliever and fever reducer if used properly, Kramer says.
Don't combine drugs that contain acetaminophen and inform your doctor if you have liver problems or drink alcohol daily, Busuttil says.
You should tell your doctor or pharmacist about all the medicines you are taking, Veltri says. Read ingredient labels and follow directions exactly. Don't use more than the maximum dose unless you have spoken to your doctor about it.

—Mary Brophy Marcus

Hepatitis can lead to disabling illness, liver cancer, liver failure, and death. Often people don't realize they are infected with hepatitis. They spread the infection to others by handling food with dirty hands, having sex without using condoms, or sharing dirty needles for drug injections.

Yet hepatitis is largely preventable. This book will cover the basics of hepatitis, including symptoms, transmission, and prevention. It provides the information you need to protect yourself, your friends, and your family from hepatitis.

# CHAPTER ONE

# HEPATITIS BASICS

Ethan, sixteen years old, went out for pizza with his friends. They celebrated the school basketball team's win at the regional championship. He started feeling a little tired a couple of weeks later but blamed it on his crazy schedule. Ethan caught the news late one night just before bedtime. The reporter talked about an outbreak of hepatitis. The reporter said that everyone who had eaten at a certain restaurant in the past two months should talk to their doctors. The reporter said those people might have hepatitis. It was the same pizza place where Ethan had celebrated with his friends.

Mai, twenty-eight years old, is pregnant with her first baby. She is due to deliver in just a few weeks. Her doctor called her into the office one day to talk about a test result. The doctor told Mai that she had hepatitis B and that she might pass it to her baby during birth. The doctor said hepatitis B spreads by sexual activity. The doctor asked about Mai's background. Mai told him that she was adopted from China when she was two years old.

Jessica, twenty-five years old, has been feeling bad for a while. She's tired, achy, and bloated. She has belly pain off and on. She made an appointment for a checkup with her doctor. The doctor ordered some blood tests. Jessica was worried, but not surprised, when the doctor said the tests showed hepatitis B. Jessica guessed that she got the virus from having sex with a man she met in a bar. It only took one night to get hepatitis B.

Charlie, fifty-five years old, has known that he has hepatitis C for ten years. He was in a bad motorcycle accident when he was a young man. At the hospital, doctors gave him a blood transfusion. Charlie was one of about three hundred thousand Americans who have gotten hepatitis C from blood transfusions. They were infected before donated *blood could be tested for the virus. Charlie's doctor tests his blood every six months. About every eighteen months, he performs a liver biopsy, a procedure in which a doctor uses a needle to take a small sample of the liver for testing. Recent tests show that Charlie's liver has early signs of permanent damage.*

*Jackson, thirty-five years old, was injecting heroin several times a week by the time he was sixteen. All he could think about was where to get his next fix and how to pay for it. Jackson was eventually arrested for theft. He went through heroin detox in the county hospital. Then he spent more than a year in juvenile detention. He's been clean since he was nineteen years old and has put the past behind him. He has a wife, two young children, and a job that he enjoys. Hepatitis is the last thing on his mind.*

Hepatitis is an inflammation of the liver. An inflammation is the body's response to injury or irritation. Think of it this way.

Hepatitis can affect anyone. No one group of people is more likely to have hepatitis than any other. Certain parts of the world have more instances of it due to poor sanitation and inadequate medical precautions.

If you accidentally hit your thumb with a hammer, it would become swollen, hot, red, and *really* sore. Your thumb would be inflamed. A few days later, perhaps you would notice some pus draining from the injury. That's a sure sign of an infection setting in. Your thumb has become both inflamed and infected. A liver suffering from viral hepatitis is also inflamed and infected. Before discussing hepatitis in detail, it's important to know a little bit more about the liver.

## MEET YOUR LIVER

The liver is unique among the body's organs. It is the only organ that can regenerate itself. This means that it is able to regrow lost or destroyed tissue. If a person's liver is injured in an accident and part of it has to be removed, it will grow back to its full size. If a mother donates part of her liver to her child, both the mother and child will eventually regrow full-sized and well-functioning livers. This partially explains why some people recover from viral hepatitis. In many cases, however, hepatitis viruses damage a liver so badly that it is permanently scarred and can no longer repair itself.

The liver is made up of cells called hepatocytes. Each of these tiny, twelve-sided cells is almost like an entire miniature liver. No single brain cell can organize a thought. No single heart cell can pump blood through the body. But each hepatocyte can carry out most of the functions required of the liver.

The average adult liver is the size of a football, but its shape is more like a lopsided triangle. The bulk of the liver is tucked up under the right rib cage for protection. One side extends across the middle of the chest behind the breastbone, or sternum. The liver rises to about the nipple line on the chest. A structure called the diaphragm separates it from the lungs.

## PLACEMENT OF LIVER AMONG
## THE OTHER ORGANS OF THE DIGESTIVE SYSTEM

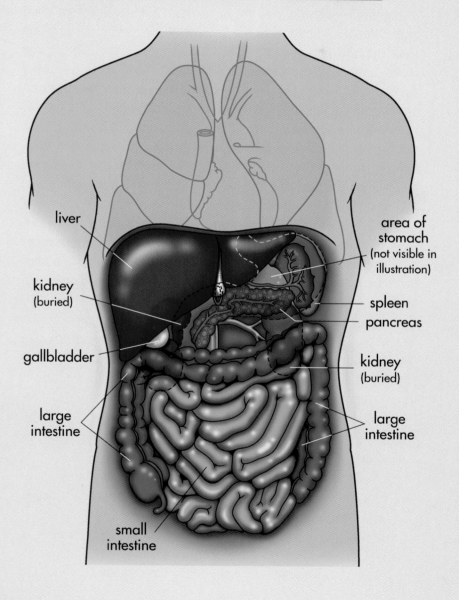

liver

area of
stomach
(not visible in
illustration)

kidney
(buried)

spleen

pancreas

gallbladder

kidney
(buried)

large
intestine

large
intestine

small
intestine

A healthy liver is smooth. It has a reddish brown color because of its plentiful blood supply. About 1.5 quarts (1,500 milliliters) of blood rush through the liver each minute. About 25 percent of the blood flows into the liver through the hepatic artery, which comes directly from the heart. The other 75 percent of the blood flowing into the liver comes through the portal vein. This vein delivers nutrient-rich blood from the intestines to the liver for processing.

Nearly everything we eat, drink, inhale, or absorb through our skin eventually travels to the liver to be processed and purified. Have you ever heard of the five-second rule? The rule says that if you drop a cookie on the floor, it's okay to eat it if you pick it up within five seconds. (You *do* know that several million germs are crawling all over the cookie by then, don't you?) Even if we don't eat cookies off the floor, much of our food is loaded with germs when we swallow it. Yet we seldom get sick from the food we eat. Most bacteria in food travel from the intestines through the portal vein to the liver, where they are destroyed.

That is just one of approximately five hundred important jobs the liver does. Think of the liver as a very busy chemical factory that is constantly producing new chemicals and recycling old ones. It also supervises a few other factories and stows spare parts for many of those factories. The liver does the following and more:

- Makes a blood protein called albumin, which helps to keep the body's fluid in balance so that the blood is not too thick or too thin
- Makes proteins that assist in the proper clotting of blood
- Stores the vitamins A, $B_{12}$, D, E, and K, and the minerals copper and iron
- Breaks down ammonia, which is created when protein is digested
- Produces bile, a substance needed to break down fatty foods

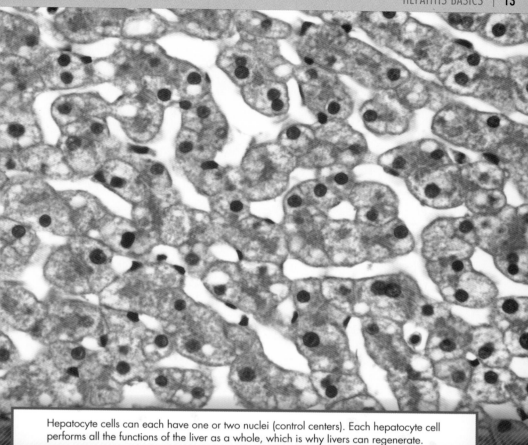

Hepatocyte cells can each have one or two nuclei (control centers). Each hepatocyte cell performs all the functions of the liver as a whole, which is why livers can regenerate.

- Collects and recycles bilirubin, a substance released by red blood cells as they age and die
- Makes cholesterol, which is needed for healthy cells
- Removes excess cholesterol from the body
- Transforms carbohydrates and sugars from food into glucose for immediate use by the body
- Processes excess glucose and stores it for future use
- Turns proteins into the amino acids needed to make muscles
- Converts many medications into a form that the body can use
- Neutralizes toxins and poisons, including alcohol, pesticides, and certain drugs

Many of the symptoms of hepatitis are directly related to the infected liver's inability to do those jobs well. For example, some people with hepatitis have yellowish skin. The whites of their eyes (called the sclera) are also yellowish. This means a person's liver is unable to properly collect and process bilirubin. Red blood cells, which have a life span of 90 to 120 days, release bilirubin when they die. This is normally taken up by the liver and added to bile, which is then excreted through the intestinal tract in stool (bile is what makes stool brown). If the liver cannot process bilirubin, it builds up in the blood and turns the skin and sclera yellow.

## A LITTLE ABOUT VIRUSES

Viruses are microscopic organisms that cause disease. Viruses are not living things. Unlike bacteria, they don't need food, water, or oxygen to survive. They also cannot move or multiply by themselves. Viruses are said to replicate rather than reproduce, because they lack the means for true reproduction. Viruses can grow and multiply only after they have entered a living cell, called a host. Humans are the host for hepatitis viruses.

Viruses are much smaller than bacteria. For example, if a single bacterium were the size of a basketball, a virus would be the size of a marble. Viruses are so small that millions of them could fit inside the period at the end of this sentence. Viruses are also much simpler than bacteria.

A number of viruses are responsible for hepatitis. The various hepatitis viruses differ from one another in some ways, but they also share several traits. First, they generally infect only hepatocytes. Bacteria, on the other hand, can infect many different parts of the body. For example, a bacteria called *Streptococcus pneumoniae* can cause pneumonia, meningitis, ear and sinus infections, and other

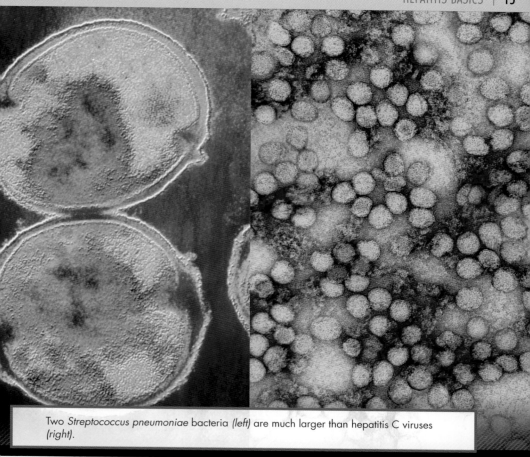

Two *Streptococcus pneumoniae* bacteria *(left)* are much larger than hepatitis C viruses *(right)*.

diseases. Hepatitis viruses cause only hepatitis. People infected with hepatitis viruses are highly contagious for days or even weeks before they realize they are sick. During this time, they can easily spread the disease to others.

Hepatitis viruses generally do not destroy the living cells in which they replicate. Instead, the original infected cell releases new viruses that move on to infect other hepatocytes. The first cell is damaged, but not destroyed. Usually, the liver can repair the damaged hepatocyte. Over a period of years, however, the overactive state of the body's immune system and the constant rebuilding of hepatocytes can cause long-term liver damage.

## Immunity and Vaccines

The human immune system protects our bodies from the millions of dangerous organisms that attack us every day. Several types of white blood cells make up the first line of defense. These vital cells circulate in the bloodstream along with red blood cells.

An immune reaction begins when microbes (living organisms so small that they can be seen only with a microscope) enter the body through a break in the skin. The invaders can also enter in food or water or by being inhaled. Our white blood cells chase down the invaders and destroy many of them.

Suppose the measles virus enters a little girl's body. White blood cells in her immune system help fight and kill much of the virus. She will get sick from the measles, but if she has a healthy immune system, she will likely recover (although measles sometimes causes serious illness and death).

## THE ABCs (AND BEYOND) OF VIRAL HEPATITIS

The ancient Greek doctor Hippocrates, who is considered to be the father of medicine, described the yellow jaundice of hepatitis. Historic documents show that hepatitis outbreaks increased during wartime, when soldiers were commonly crowded together. This evidence convinced doctors that hepatitis was an infectious disease. During World War II (1939–1945), hepatitis outbreaks occurred after soldiers were vaccinated for measles and yellow fever. The doctors passed the virus on when they used one needle to inject several people.

After the child gets measles, her body's second line of defense kicks into action. Her immune system makes antibodies against the measles virus. If the measles virus attacks the girl again, her immune system will remember the virus and send out anti-measles antibodies to fight off the infection. The girl will not get sick this time because she has become immune to measles.

In some cases, we don't have to get sick from a disease to become immune to it. That's where vaccines come in. Vaccines are medications made from killed or weakened microbes. Doctors or nurses usually inject patients with vaccines, although some can be swallowed or inhaled. Inside the body, vaccines stimulate the immune system to form antibodies against certain kinds of microbes.

Suppose that a little boy has never had measles. Instead, he receives the measles vaccine when he is very young. His body makes antibodies against measles. If he is exposed to measles in the future, he will not get sick. He is immune to measles.

Scientists have identified seven hepatitis viruses and named them alphabetically (hepatitis A through G). Hepatitis viruses A, B, and C are the most common causes of hepatitis in the United States. There may be additional hepatitis viruses that are yet to be discovered.

## HEPATITIS A

Identified in 1973, the hepatitis A virus infects thousands of Americans each year. It generally causes a fairly mild form of the disease. People usually recover without any long-lasting problems. Hepatitis A is primarily passed via the oral-fecal route, which means

the virus is in the feces (stool) of infected people. Infected people can pass hepatitis A to others when they handle food or dishes without washing their hands thoroughly after going to the bathroom. A vaccine that protects against hepatitis A is available.

## HEPATITIS B

This virus was identified in 1963. About 1.25 million Americans have hepatitis B. Up to 5 percent of the people on Earth might be infected with hepatitis B at any given time. Many people recover without treatment, but some develop a more serious, long-lasting illness. They may require extensive treatment or even a liver transplant. The hepatitis B virus can live on surfaces (such as dishes, doorknobs, bathroom fixtures, and countertops) for three days or more. Hepatitis B spreads mainly through sexual contact. The virus can be found in bodily fluids such as semen, saliva, blood, and tears. A hepatitis B vaccine is available.

## HEPATITIS C

Identified in 1989, hepatitis C is four times more common in the United States than human immunodeficiency virus (HIV)/AIDS. Hepatitis C mainly spreads via infected blood. Blood can pass from one person to another when people share dirty needles for drug injection. In the past, hepatitis C sometimes passed from one person to another via blood transfusions. People with hepatitis C infections can go for many years without noticing any symptoms. During this time, they might pass hepatitis C to other people. About 70 percent of people with hepatitis C do not realize they have it. Treatment of hepatitis C is grueling and carries major side effects. As with hepatitis B, some people with hepatitis C require liver transplants. This form of hepatitis is the primary cause of liver cancer. There is no vaccine to prevent hepatitis C.

**March 10, 2008**

From the Pages of USA TODAY

# Adult vaccines make a point:
# Vaccines are not just for kids anymore

Depending on health history, age and other risk factors, adults may benefit from vaccines for:

Influenza
Pneumococcal disease
Hepatitis A & B
Whooping cough

Shingles
Human papillomavirus (HPV)
Meningococcal disease

*—Kim Painter*

## HEPATITIS D

Identified in 1977, hepatitis D infection can occur only in a person who is already infected with hepatitis B. The hepatitis D virus is also called the delta agent. It is like a parasite that preys on another virus. It needs the genetic material of the hepatitis B virus to replicate. Patients infected with the hepatitis B and D viruses at the same time are much sicker than patients who are infected with hepatitis B alone. Such people can become suddenly and seriously ill. Up to 20 percent of people with hepatitis B and D will die. Hepatitis D spreads through sexual contact or sometimes via blood.

## HEPATITIS E, F, AND G

Identified in 1990, the hepatitis E virus is responsible for very large outbreaks of hepatitis. For example, up to twenty thousand cases of hepatitis E occur each year in Katmandu, Nepal, a nation in southern Asia.

USA TODAY

www.usatoday.com

USA TODAY

Life

SECTION D

June 30, 2003

From the Pages of USA TODAY

# Safety rules drain blood banks: As new diseases arise, the screening process grows, and more donors are turned away

Blood banks have long struggled to meet the high demand for blood, but they fear that a wave of new regulations that prohibit many categories of Americans from donating could result in major shortages.

As diseases like SARS [severe acute respiratory syndrome] and West Nile emerge, posing potential threats to Americans and their blood supply, the number of screening tests performed on blood and the restrictions on donors have grown. [In 2003] blood labs started using a new, experimental test to detect West Nile virus in donated blood. They already tested for HIV, a form of leukemia, hepatitis B and C and syphilis. In addition, the list of questions about health, travel and sexual history that can disqualify donors burgeoned to nearly 50, up from about 15 in the era before HIV.

The result of all the new restrictions, many of them imposed in 2002–2003: Blood banks can't accept donations from people who lived in England for three months between 1980 and 1996 or in

Europe for five years since 1980 [because of the fear of mad cow disease]. You can't give blood if you had a fever with headache in the last week, or if you had been in a place affected by SARS.

Blood is and must remain safe, blood bank directors say, but they worry that an excess of caution will create serious shortages.

"With every new question, every new test, we always end up deferring more donors," says Nora Hirschler, president of Blood Centers of the Pacific.

At a time when the blood supply is "always on edge," every eligible donor is needed, says Mike Strong, vice president of the Puget Sound Blood Center in Seattle. "They keep putting more and more hurdles in front of us, and unfortunately, many people don't want to give blood anyway."

The Food and Drug Administration regulates blood donations. It requires donor restrictions, which it calls "deferrals," to reduce the risk that diseases might be passed from person to person by way of transfusion. Regulators are following the lessons of the 1980s, when the blood industry's failure to address the risk of AIDS resulted in 20,000 people becoming infected with HIV through transfusions.

—*Anita Manning*

### Who cannot donate blood

Every potential blood donor must answer nearly 50 questions before he or she is allowed to donate. Among the reasons for disqualifying someone from giving blood:

- If you weigh less than 110 pounds [50 kg].
- If you're under 17 years old (though 16-year-olds can donate with written permission of a parent or guardian).
- If you have injected yourself with drugs not prescribed by a doctor.
- If you have a history of hepatitis or a positive lab test for the virus.
- If you have a blood-related cancer such as Hodgkin's disease, leukemia, or lymphoma.
- If you have had chemotherapy or radiation for cancer within a year.
- If you have symptoms or laboratory evidence of an HIV infection.
- If you have had gonorrhea within a year.
- If you have had angina, a heart attack, angioplasty or bypass surgery within a year.
- For males, if you have had sex with another man since 1977.
- For females, if you have had sex within the past year with a man who had sex with another man since 1977.
- If you have visited or lived in England, Scotland, Wales or Northern Ireland for 3 months or more from 1980 through 1996.
- If you have lived five years or more, cumulatively, in Europe since 1980.
- If, as a military person, dependent or a civilian, you have spent six months or more between 1980 and 1996 on a military base in Belgium, the Netherlands, Germany, Spain, Portugal, Turkey, Italy or Greece.
- If you emigrated from a malaria-affected area less than three years ago.
- If you have had a tattoo within a year.
- If you have taken Accutane, an acne medicine, within a month.

Unsanitary conditions such as these in New Delhi, India, make the transmission of hepatitis A and E much more prevalent.

Hepatitis E is usually found in water that is contaminated by human feces. Like hepatitis A, it spreads through the oral-fecal route. It is rarely seen in the United States. Hepatitis E causes mild disease in children but is more dangerous in adults. On average, about 20 percent of pregnant women infected with hepatitis E die during their pregnancy.

A few cases of hepatitis F were reported in the past. These are now classified as hepatitis C.

Identified in 1995, hepatitis G occurs around the world. It causes a wide range of illness, from mild, flulike symptoms to serious illness or death. Hepatitis G passes via blood and bodily fluids.

# The Types of Viral Hepatitis

| VIRUS | PRIMARY MODE OF TRANSMISSION | ACUTE/ CHRONIC DISEASE | VACCINE | EFFECTIVE TREATMENT |
|---|---|---|---|---|
| A | Food and water, oral-fecal route | Acute | Yes | No |
| B | Sex, infected blood, intravenous drug use | Acute and chronic | Yes | Yes |
| C | Infected blood, sex | Acute and chronic | No | Yes |
| D | Sex, infected blood, intravenous drug use | Acute and chronic | No | Yes |
| E | Contaminated water | Acute | No | No |
| G | Infected blood, sex | Acute and chronic | No | No |

*Note: Hepatitis D only occurs simultaneously with B virus.

# NONINFECTIOUS HEPATITIS

A few things can cause liver inflammation without liver infection. This condition is called noninfectious hepatitis. The most common cause of noninfectious hepatitis in the United States is nonalcoholic fatty liver. Just as extra pounds of fat build up on the thighs and hips, they can build up on internal organs, such as the heart and the liver. Most people with nonalcoholic fatty liver disease are overweight or obese. Some have high cholesterol. Having type 2 diabetes, a disease in which the body is resistant to insulin, increases the risk for this type of hepatitis. This is because type 2 diabetes is closely linked with being overweight or obese. The heavier the person, the more likely he or she is to have type 2 diabetes, high cholesterol, and nonalcoholic fatty liver disease. An estimated 3 percent of the U.S. population has hepatitis due to nonalcoholic fatty liver disease.

Another form of noninfectious hepatitis is called autoimmune hepatitis. This is a condition in which the body's immune system attacks the liver. It is relatively rare, affecting about one hundred thousand to two hundred thousand people in the United States at any given time. About 70 percent of people with this form of hepatitis are women. The majority of them are between the ages of fifteen and forty. There is no cure for autoimmune hepatitis, but there are treatments to help control it. Some people with this condition may need a liver transplant, but donor livers are hard to find. Many people who need a liver transplant never receive one.

Certain medications and toxins (poisons) cause another form of noninfectious hepatitis. For example, people with liver problems may further damage their liver with acetaminophen. This medication is found in numerous over-the-counter remedies for headaches, colds, and the flu. Occasionally, prescription medications may damage the liver. These medications include isoniazid (used to treat tuberculosis), phenytoin (used to prevent seizures), diazepam (used for anxiety), tamoxifen (used to treat breast cancer), and halothane (an inhaled gas used to put people to sleep during surgery).

Other toxins that can damage the liver include certain poisonous mushrooms; pesticides; and carbon tetrachloride, a chemical once used to dry-clean clothing. For some people, stopping the medication or avoiding the toxin allows the liver to regenerate. The liver damage is permanent in other people. In the United States, such toxins and medications are responsible for about 10 percent of all cases of noninfectious hepatitis.

Nonalcoholic fatty liver makes the liver appear yellow *(right)*, whereas a healthy liver will be reddish brown *(left)*.

USA TODAY

www.usatoday.com

**Life**
SECTION D

March 1, 2007

From the Pages of USA TODAY

# Obesity's cycle of vulnerability: As adults, excess weight may render drugs toxic

Being obese or having a high-fat diet may make people more sensitive to drugs that aren't toxic in thin people, put them at a higher risk for cancer and even increase their risk of death from using illegal drugs, a panel of researchers says.

That's on top of the difficulty of finding the right medication dose for heavy patients.

With many drugs, the dose is based on lean body mass (muscle, bone and other non-fat tissue), which can be so challenging to calculate in obese patients "that the adjustment usually is not appropriately made," says George Corcoran, chair of pharmaceutical sciences at Wayne State University in Detroit and chairman of the panel at this year's American Association

## ACUTE AND CHRONIC INFECTION

Doctors look at hepatitis in two ways. First, they consider the cause. Is it one of the known hepatitis viruses, obesity, high cholesterol, an autoimmune condition, or a response to a medication or a toxic substance? Second, they consider how long a person has had hepatitis. Knowing how long someone has been sick with hepatitis helps doctors plan the most helpful treatment. Doctors describe hepatitis as being acute, chronic, or fulminant, which means a condition with a rapid onset and unusually severe symptoms.

People with acute hepatitis have been sick for less than six months. They may be mildly ill or very sick. Because of the strength of the human immune system and the liver's amazing power to for the Advancement of Science meeting.

Not only do clinicians have to find the right dose, but they also must contend with a body that may more readily convert that drug to a dangerous substance, Corcoran says. "It's a one-two whammy."

And even if the dose is right, it could cause problems. With both prescription and over-the-counter drugs, numerous studies show that rats that are fed a high-fat diet are more prone to liver and kidney damage. The drugs discussed included acetaminophen, the diuretic furosemide and certain powerful antibiotics in the aminoglycoside family, Corcoran says.

The acetaminophen link is especially troubling because half of all the liver transplants in the USA are the result of acetaminophen toxicity leading to liver failure, he says.

In the case of liver damage, the problem appears to be that a high-fat diet or obesity produces changes in liver enzymes. These enzymes are proteins that metabolize substances coming into the body.

So in the body of an obese person, drugs can be more toxic than in a lean person because the enzymes that do the work are different, Corcoran says. Studies in humans, mice and rats have shown this to be the case. These findings could explain why obese people have higher rates of liver and kidney disease, he says.

In the obese, the liver is often already damaged by the presence of excess fat in liver cells, according to researchers at the Mayo Clinic. And damaged livers may be more susceptible to injuries from drugs and chemicals, Corcoran says.

*—Elizabeth Weise*

repair itself, many people recover completely from hepatitis in less than six months. The symptoms of acute hepatitis come on quickly, usually within a few weeks of infection. Then the symptoms gradually disappear, and the person experiences a complete recovery. The inflammation subsides, and the immune system destroys all the hepatitis viruses. In most cases, the liver does not suffer permanent damage with acute hepatitis.

In some cases, acute hepatitis progresses to chronic hepatitis, or hepatitis that lasts longer than six months. People with chronic hepatitis may be sick for years without knowing it. Or they may be only mildly ill every now and then. This is why people infected with chronic hepatitis can pass the virus to others without knowing it.

Eventually, most people with chronic hepatitis do become ill, but it may take as long as twenty to thirty years for symptoms to appear.

When someone has chronic hepatitis, liver damage may progress to cirrhosis. This is a condition in which the liver is badly scarred. The damage is irreversible. Cirrhosis is caused by a process called fibrosis, in which tough connective tissue grows in the liver. This tissue damages or even destroys hepatocytes. Virtually any kind of chronic liver disease, including hepatitis, can cause cirrhosis. In the United States, excess alcohol intake is the leading cause of cirrhosis. Worldwide, viral hepatitis is the leading cause.

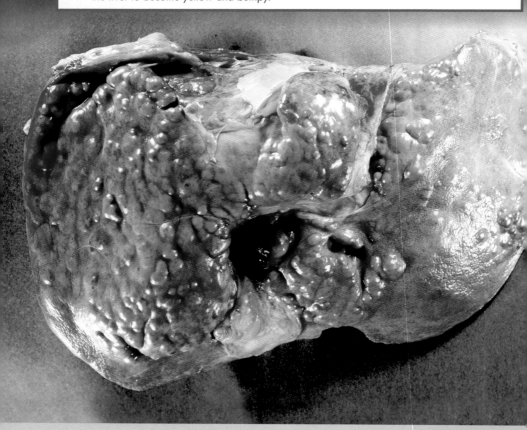

This human liver has been destroyed by cirrhosis and hepatitis. The cirrhosis causes the liver to become yellow and bumpy.

Rarely, acute hepatitis progresses to fulminant hepatitis. In fulminant hepatitis, the liver fails suddenly, often within eight weeks of the onset of illness. The liver is unlikely to regenerate. Often a liver transplant is necessary. As many as eight out of ten people with fulminant hepatitis die if they do not receive a liver transplant.

This book focuses on infectious hepatitis caused by the A, B, and C viruses. The symptoms of hepatitis are remarkably similar regardless of which virus attacks the liver. The things that differ are how an individual becomes infected, the incubation period, the treatment, and the expected outcome.

# CHAPTER TWO

# SYMPTOMS AND DIAGNOSIS OF HEPATITIS

Jessica worried that she might have AIDS. She was tired and sometimes had pain in her abdomen. Jessica missed classes at the community college she attended and missed the last two days of her job at the bookstore. She went to the college clinic to see the doctor for an AIDS test. The doctor told Jessica that her blood tests showed she was negative for HIV but that she had hepatitis B.

Some people discover that they have hepatitis by accident. Suppose you visit your doctor for a routine physical exam. A couple of weeks later, the doctor asks you to return to the office to discuss some abnormal blood tests. She says that you have hepatitis. Or maybe you want to donate blood to the local blood bank because your friend is having surgery. The blood bank takes a small sample of your blood and tests it for hepatitis, HIV (the virus that causes AIDS), and several other diseases. The nurse at the blood bank says you cannot donate blood because the test shows that you have hepatitis or had it in the past.

Other people learn that they have been exposed to hepatitis and need to find out if they have been infected. A college student might call his girlfriend, telling her that he has hepatitis and she needs to be tested for it. Or a mother of twins finds out that several cases of hepatitis were reported at the day care center her children attend. All children who attend that day care center must see their doctors right away.

Some people discover they have hepatitis because they have symptoms. For example, a man notices that the whites of his eyes are yellowish and his urine is brown. He drives to an urgent care clinic for an immediate examination. The symptoms for all types of

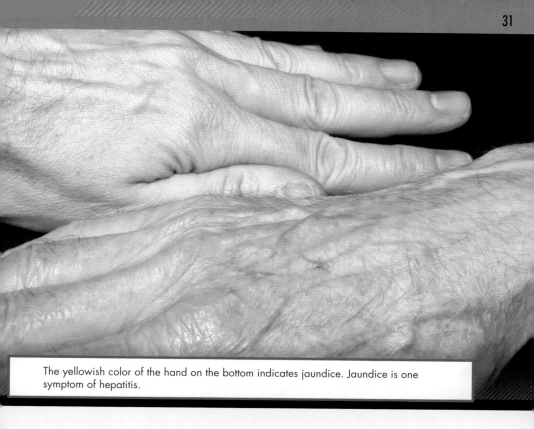

The yellowish color of the hand on the bottom indicates jaundice. Jaundice is one symptom of hepatitis.

hepatitis are similar. Doctors use the same tests to diagnose all of them. Only a few specialized blood tests can identify the specific hepatitis virus.

## SYMPTOMS OF HEPATITIS

The liver isn't big on complaining. It just keeps on repairing itself and doing its job for as long as possible. People may live with hepatitis for years without experiencing any symptoms. In fact, someone can have advanced hepatitis without being aware of it. In contrast, if a child shows up in the emergency room (ER) with a fever, stiff neck, headache, and confusion, the ER doctor can be fairly certain that the child has meningitis. If a man goes to the ER with crushing chest pain, shortness of breath, and an irregular heartbeat, the doctor will suspect that the man is having a heart attack.

But the symptoms of hepatitis can be vague or nonspecific. They are similar to symptoms of diseases ranging from the common cold to cancer. Symptoms include fatigue, flulike symptoms, pain, and jaundice. Some people will experience all of them, but others will have none or just a few.

Fatigue is the most common sign of hepatitis. We all get tired from time to time, but fatigue goes way beyond that. A fatigued man may have trouble getting out of bed in the morning. He may be so tired that he cannot go to work. A woman might feel as if she's run a marathon after doing a little gardening. She must return to bed for a long nap. Fatigue can upset a person's daily routine.

During the acute stages of hepatitis, people may feel as if they have the flu. Their symptoms might include muscle and joint pain, headaches, weakness, nausea, and loss of appetite. A few people may have a mild fever as well. In someone with chronic hepatitis, these symptoms may come and go over a long period. Occasionally, people with acute hepatitis feel a mild tenderness, fullness, or discomfort in the right upper quadrant, or quarter, of the abdomen.

Jaundice may be the first sign that someone has hepatitis. When the damaged liver cannot collect and recycle bilirubin, the excess of this yellowish pigment collects in the sclera and skin. The sclera and skin become yellowish when someone is jaundiced. Surplus bilirubin also collects in the urine, turning it a brownish color. When someone is jaundiced, his or her stool becomes light beige. Jaundice can also be a sign of serious liver deterioration.

Abnormal itching is called pruritus. It is a clue that something is wrong with the liver. The itching can be mild or so intense that it prevents someone from going to school or even sleeping. The abnormal flow of bile within the liver is the cause of the itching. Unfortunately, scratching does not relieve the itchiness, and excessive scratching can lead to infection. Medications may help pruritus, but they do not eliminate it.

A damaged liver cannot break down ammonia, a harmful by-product of protein digestion. With too much ammonia in the body, people can become forgetful, confused, or sleepy. Doctors call this hepatic encephalopathy. It can progress to coma and even death.

Some people with hepatitis are not able to digest or absorb their food properly because the liver is not working well. Their intestines fill with gas, and the abdomen is bloated and uncomfortable.

People with severe liver disease may hold as much as 1 to 1.5 gallons (4–6 liters) of excess fluid in their abdomen. This collection of fluid in the abdomen is called ascites. Ascites distends the abdomen and can be very unpleasant or even painful. Other physical signs include excess fluid buildup in the ankles and feet and a loss of firm muscle mass (called muscle wasting) in the upper body.

Hepatitis can interfere with the liver's ability to produce substances that control blood clotting. This can result in easy bruising, bleeding from the gums, or excessive bleeding from a minor cut. In some cases, rectal bleeding can occur or blood might be seen in the stool.

Hepatitis can also have psychological effects. It is common for people with any serious or chronic illness to be depressed. People with hepatitis may become depressed because they are badly fatigued, itchy, or uncomfortable. Someone with mild encephalopathy may be depressed because his or her mental functions are declining. Once recognized, depression can often be addressed with therapy and medications.

## DIAGNOSING HEPATITIS

Most people don't know they have hepatitis when they go to the doctor. They just know they don't feel quite right. Maybe they've had one or more symptoms, such as fatigue or a bit of nausea and bloating. When someone shows up at a doctor's office with a possible illness, the doctor follows a systematic process for arriving at a diagnosis. It begins with taking a medical history and doing a physical examination. Health-care workers call this process the H&P (history and physical).

## THE H&P

The doctor or perhaps a nurse or physician's assistant takes a detailed medical history. Some of the questions may seem irrelevant, and some are very personal. However, it is important for the patient to tell the doctor the truth. Otherwise, the doctor may reach an incorrect diagnosis.

Health-care workers seldom judge people for what they did in the past. Many of us have a secret or two that we don't want other people to know about. A middle-aged businessman might have injected drugs for a few months when he was in his twenties. Yet

A doctor or nurse always begins a visit with a discussion of the patient's medical history and symptoms.

it's vital for a doctor to know these facts when considering the possibility of hepatitis. Nurses and doctors cannot gossip about patients because strict laws protect patients' privacy. People can feel safe when sharing personal information with doctors and nurses.

A doctor may ask dozens of questions while taking a complete medical history. If hepatitis is suspected, these questions might include the following:

- What brought you in to see me today?
- What are your symptoms? How long have they lasted? Are they getting better or worse?
- Have you or anyone in your family ever had liver problems?
- Have you ever received a blood transfusion or been told that you cannot donate blood?
- Do you have any body piercings or tattoos?
- How much alcohol do you drink, and how long have you been drinking alcohol?
- Have you ever injected drugs?
- What are your sexual activities and sexual orientation?
- Have you recently traveled outside the United States?
- Did you ever serve in the military?
- What is your usual diet like? Have you lost or gained weight recently?
- Have you noticed any unusual bruising or seen blood in your stool?
- Do you work around any toxic substances such as pesticides, paint thinners, or other chemicals?
- What is your past medical history? Have you had any operations for which you received anesthesia?
- What prescription medications do you take?
- What over-the-counter medications or herbal remedies do you use?

www.usatoday.com

USA TODAY

Life
SECTION D

December 19, 2005

From the Pages of USA TODAY

# Will the sins of your past catch up with you?

Many of us begin taking care of our bodies only after they start to ache, leading the older, wiser—and recently virtuous—among us to ask: Is it too late to undo the damage caused by all that fun? USA TODAY's Liz Szabo asked leading medical experts for their advice.

## The risks
### SEX

**How can people protect themselves in the future?**

In addition to unplanned pregnancies, unsafe sex can spread viruses that cause AIDS, cervical cancer and hepatitis B and C.

**Can the harm be undone?**

In some cases the immune system eventually fights off most infections of the human papillomavirus, or HPV, which can lead to cervical cancer, says Charlotte Gaydos, an associate professor of medicine at Johns Hopkins School of Medicine [in Maryland]. Bacterial infections such as syphilis, gonorrhea and chlamydia can be cured with antibiotics. Although abstinence and monogamy are the safest strategies, condoms also greatly reduce the risk, says David Soper, professor of obstetrics and gynecology at the Medical University of South Carolina-Charleston.

**Can disease be detected and treated?**

Yes. People with symptoms should see their doctors, who also can test for "silent" infections that may not cause symptoms, such as HIV, HPV and chlamydia, Gaydos says. She encourages women to undergo annual Pap tests, which can detect cervical cancer early, when it is more

The physical examination is the second half of the H&P. It's important to remember that the doctor may not find anything unusual during the physical exam even if the patient has hepatitis. The nurse or physician's assistant will weigh the patient and take easily treated and cured. People who are treated for HIV can live for years with the disease and are also less likely to spread the virus.

## DRUGS

**Illegal substances.** Drug use can create a number of immediate health hazards, from car accidents to strokes, says Murray Mittleman, an associate professor at Harvard Medical School [in Massachusetts]. Intravenous drug use can spread HIV and hepatitis. In the long run, habitual marijuana users face many of the same risks as cigarette smokers, such as cardiovascular disease, Mittleman says.

**Can the harm be undone?**
Some injuries, such as scarring of the arteries caused by cocaine, are irreversible, Mittleman says.

**Alcohol.** Heavy drinking can scar the liver. Alcohol use may lead to "brain shrinkage," says Ken Mukamal, an assistant professor at Harvard Medical School. The more people drink, the more brain tissue appears to waste away. Senior citizens with significant brain shrinkage tend to have more cognitive problems than others. Although even moderate alcohol use can lead to brain shrinkage, scientists don't yet know whether light drinking causes problems that would actually be noticeable.

**Can the harm be undone?**
Yes. Alcohol appears to damage brain cells, rather than kill them. People who reduce their drinking can reverse brain shrinkage, Mukamal says. The best strategy, according to the Centers for Disease Control and Prevention [in Georgia], is to avoid drugs and tobacco and to consume alcohol in moderation, if at all.

**Can disease be detected and treated?**
Rick Kellerman, president-elect of the American Academy of Family Physicians, encourages people to be honest with their doctors. A middle-aged person who drank or experimented with drugs in college, but who has had no health symptoms since then, may not need any special testing. But Harlan Krumholz, a professor of medicine, epidemiology and public health at Yale University School of Medicine [in Connecticut], says everyone could benefit from regular checkups to monitor blood pressure and other vital signs.

*—Liz Szabo*

vital signs (blood pressure, temperature, pulse, and respirations). The doctor will then check the patient's appearance for obvious signs of hepatitis. These signs can include jaundice; excess fluid in the ankles and feet; and signs of a loss of firm muscle mass,

Palpation is useful in checking for an unhealthy liver.

especially in the upper body.

The doctor will next examine the patient's abdomen. Signs of hepatitis include an abdomen swollen with gas or full of fluid, as in ascites. The doctor will check the right upper quadrant near the liver by pressing firmly with the fingertips. This is a technique called palpation. A healthy liver generally cannot be felt, because it is under the lower right rib cage. An inflamed liver may protrude below the rib cage. Its edge might feel hard or knobby. Next, the doctor will palpate the left upper quadrant where the spleen is found. Like the liver, the spleen cannot usually be palpated. However, the spleen is commonly enlarged when the liver is affected by hepatitis or other diseases.

## BLOOD WORK

It is possible that the doctor will find nothing in the H&P to suggest any specific signs of hepatitis. The next step in the examination is to run blood tests. The doctor sends the patient to a laboratory, where a phlebotomist (someone trained to draw blood) reviews the doctor's orders.

Depending on how many tests the doctor wants, the phlebotomist might need to take several vials of blood. Even if this is the case, only one needle insertion is needed. While that may seem like a lot of blood, it is not enough to make someone weak or to cause any other problems. Hepatitis is diagnosed with the following blood tests:

- Bilirubin: An elevated level of bilirubin in the blood may signal hepatitis, as well as other liver diseases.
- Albumin: A lower-than-normal level of this important protein may indicate poor nutrition, as well as hepatitis and a number of other diseases.
- PT: Prothrombin time (PT) is the time it takes for blood to clot in a test tube. Normally it takes less than thirteen seconds. Vitamin K ensures that blood clots form properly. If the liver is damaged or if it cannot store enough vitamin K, it may take two or three times longer than normal for blood to clot. This situation may lead to easy bruising and bleeding in the intestinal tract.

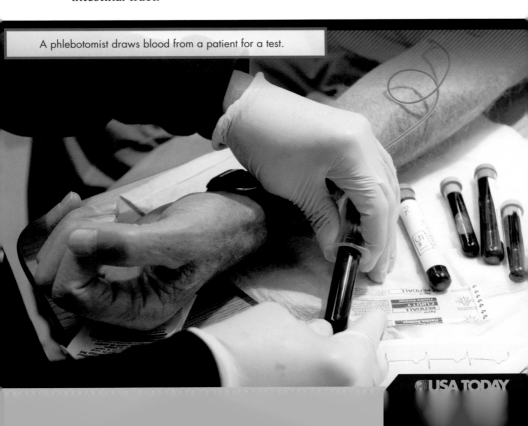

A phlebotomist draws blood from a patient for a test.

USA TODAY

www.usatoday.com

USA TODAY

**Life**

SECTION D

**March 25, 1997**

From the Pages of USA TODAY

# Identifying hepatitis C, the virulent "silent disease"

IN SEARCH OF CAUSES AND A CURE Hepatitis C virus, acquired years before it causes symptoms, can lead to debilitating fatigue, cirrhosis, liver cancer and death. Doctors can't predict with certainty how it will progress in any individual. Until 1989, doctors had no test to identify hepatitis C. They knew something was there but called it "non-A, non-B" hepatitis. Once a test became available, blood banks began screening for it. But anyone who got a transfusion before 1990 is at risk.

Also at risk are people who have tattoos or pierced body parts, have ever injected drugs, snorted cocaine, shared personal items such as razors or toothbrushes or undergone kidney dialysis.

"This is a silent disease until it reaches a certain point, when it's very serious," says Raymond Koff, chairman of the department of medicine and chief

- ANA: The antinuclear antibody (ANA) test detects autoimmune hepatitis and other autoimmune diseases, such as rheumatoid arthritis.
- Hepatitis virus studies: These tests measure hepatitis antigens and antibodies. An antigen is a substance foreign to the body, such as the proteins that make up bacteria, viruses, and pollen. When an antigen is introduced into the body, the immune system produces antibodies to fight it. By studying antigens and antibodies, doctors can identify which type of hepatitis a person has. The presence of antigens and antibodies can indicate current or past infection.
- Tests to examine liver enzymes. Enzymes are proteins that

of the hepatology section at Columbia MetroWest Medical Center, Framingham, Mass. It's usually detected when routine blood tests show abnormalities in liver enzymes or when someone tries to donate blood.

"People can go for a long period with no symptoms, and then they're astounded when they find out," says Koff. "Typically, you'll have a 45-year-old who is feeling quite well, going for the first time to donate blood and then getting a letter saying we can't use your blood."

Once a test became available and doctors began to look for the virus, "It became clear this was a major cause of liver disease," says Jay Hoofnagle of the National Institute of Diabetes and Digestive and Kidney Diseases at NIH [National Institutes of Health]. It is the most common cause of hepatitis and is the leading cause of liver transplants.

Hepatitis C, which causes ongoing injury to the cells of the liver through inflammation, damages not only the patient but the whole family, says Sue Duffy of Philadelphia.

Her husband, Michael, is the one who is ill, "but his disease is my disease," she says. "The worry, the not knowing what the future will hold, the change in lifestyle, the naps all day long."

Major symptoms, she says, are "overwhelming fatigue, body pain and a very high rate of depression. With a person in that condition, it can't help but affect the entire family unit."

And there is the stigma. Because hepatitis C is associated with drug use, "many people decide not to share the diagnosis, even with their family," Duffy says.

—Anita Manning

speed up chemical reactions in the body. Changes in the enzyme levels can indicate hepatitis.

People can take a simple home test called the Hepatitis C Check. The U.S. Food and Drug Administration (FDA) approved this test. The test kit includes a lancet, a small pointed device for sticking a finger, and a plastic receptacle that holds a drop or two of blood. This blood sample is mailed to a laboratory for analysis. It usually takes about ten days to get the test results. Much like at-home HIV tests, results are confidential. The tests are coded so that only the person who supplied the sample can obtain the result. The test does not replace medical care but serves as a screening tool. People who

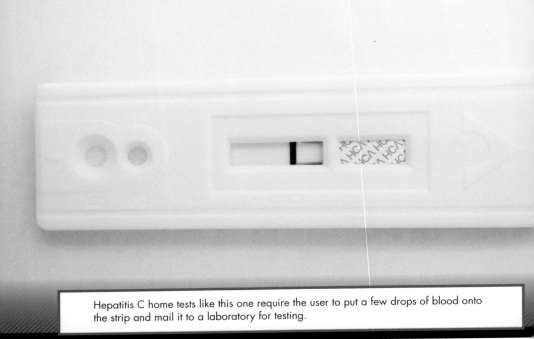

Hepatitis C home tests like this one require the user to put a few drops of blood onto the strip and mail it to a laboratory for testing.

test positive for hepatitis C should immediately see their doctors for further testing and follow-up care.

## IMAGING STUDIES

Imaging studies are medical procedures that produce pictures of parts of the body. Examples of imaging studies are sonograms and X-rays.

Sonograms (ultrasounds) are the most commonly used imaging studies to help detect liver disease. A sonogram is a painless test. A machine sends sound waves through the abdomen. The sound waves bounce off the liver and create an image on a screen. During the procedure, a technician smears a small amount of a clear gel over the abdomen. Next, the technician slides an instrument called a transducer across the abdomen. The transducer transmits pictures of the liver to a small video screen. The doctor studies printouts of the images.

Computed tomography (CT) scans and magnetic resonance imaging (MRI) are more complex imaging techniques. Both of these techniques produce excellent images of cross sections of the liver and the organs that surround it. These scans check for the presence of tumors or other liver problems. Ruling out possible problems is an important step toward making a diagnosis.

## LIVER BIOPSY

Sooner or later, many patients with viral hepatitis will need a liver biopsy. During a biopsy, a doctor takes a small piece of tissue from the liver. A biopsy is the most accurate way to identify exactly what is going on inside the liver. The biopsy result tells the doctor just how

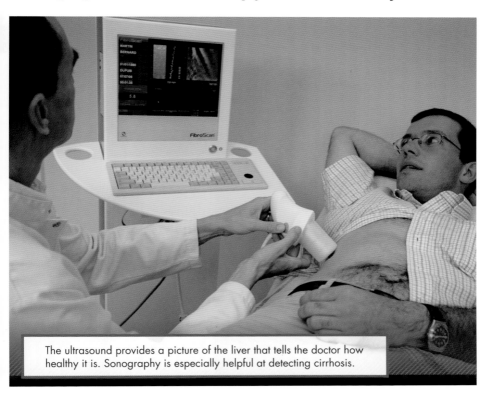

The ultrasound provides a picture of the liver that tells the doctor how healthy it is. Sonography is especially helpful at detecting cirrhosis.

badly injured or scarred the liver is. Doctors often use biopsies to determine liver damage caused by chronic hepatitis.

Patients usually receive a mild sedative before a biopsy procedure. During a liver biopsy, the patient lies on his or her back with the right arm behind the head. This position helps pull the rib cage upward and makes the liver easier to locate. A doctor may use a sonogram to precisely locate the liver. Next, the doctor injects a small amount of local anesthetic (painkiller) into the skin, similar to what a dentist uses when working on a cavity. The doctor inserts a larger, hollow biopsy needle through the numbed skin and into the liver. The hollow needle captures and withdraws a string-sized piece of tissue that is about 1 inch (2.5 centimeters) long.

While liver biopsies are generally safe, they do carry some risk. Complications can include pain, puncture of another organ (for example, the intestine), and infection. Patients must lie quietly in bed for several hours after the procedure to reduce bleeding. Death due to bleeding, which is rare, is the most serious complication of a liver biopsy. The tissue sample

This illustration shows a liver biopsy. The needle is inserted between the ribs *(they appear as oval sponges at left)* to remove part of the liver tissue.

is sent to a lab for examination by a specialist called a pathologist. The pathologist examines the samples of liver tissue to make a diagnosis.

It may take a week or so before the patient receives the test results. The patient and a family member usually return to the doctor's office to discuss the results in person and to plan future treatment. There's a lot to decide, because different types of viral hepatitis have different treatments and different outcomes.

*After blood tests confirmed that Jessica was suffering from hepatitis B, her doctor referred her to a liver specialist. He estimated that she had been infected about three months earlier. The doctor couldn't say whether Jessica's acute hepatitis would go away on its own or persist to become chronic hepatitis. By the time Jessica visited the liver specialist, she was jaundiced. Her skin was slightly yellow, and her urine was dark brown. The liver specialist advised Jessica to drop out of college for the rest of the term so she could rest and try to heal. She would have to see him once a month for the next few months. If after six months Jessica had not recovered, she would probably need to have a liver biopsy.*

# CHAPTER THREE

# HEPATITIS A

Y ou'd think it'd be safe to go out for pizza," Ethan told his friends. "I mean, you never expect to come down with hepatitis just by eating a few slices of pepperoni!" The local newspaper and television stations were all talking about the big hepatitis A outbreak linked to the pizza restaurant where Ethan had eaten a month earlier. Although Ethan was feeling tired, he didn't have any other symptoms. Still, his mom took him to the family doctor. County health officials said that everyone who had eaten at the restaurant should see their doctors to find out if they had become infected with hepatitis A.

Hepatitis A strikes an estimated 1.4 million people worldwide each year. The World Health Organization (WHO) estimates the global cost of treating hepatitis A to be between $1.5 billion and $3 billion annually. The Centers for Disease Control and Prevention (CDC) estimates that about thirty-two thousand Americans develop hepatitis A each year.

This micrograph of hepatitis A has been colorized to better show the virus. It is magnified about 150,000 times its actual size.

Before the hepatitis A vaccine became available, an estimated 380,000 cases of hepatitis A occurred each year in the United States. Hepatitis A is so common that about one-third of Americans test positive for it, meaning they have had it in the past or are infected with it.

Hepatitis A is caused by the hepatovirus, a virus in the family of picornaviruses. Viruses in the same family include the rhinoviruses, which cause the common cold. Enteroviruses, which include the virus that causes the common childhood illness known as hand, foot, and mouth disease, are also in this family of viruses. Humans are the only natural host for the hepatitis A virus. However, primates such as chimpanzees and monkeys can catch the virus from people and then transmit it to other people. This transmission could happen, for example, in zoos or other places where primates and people are in close contact.

This map from the World Health Organization shows countries and areas at risk for hepatitis A.

## Hepatitis A, countries or areas at risk

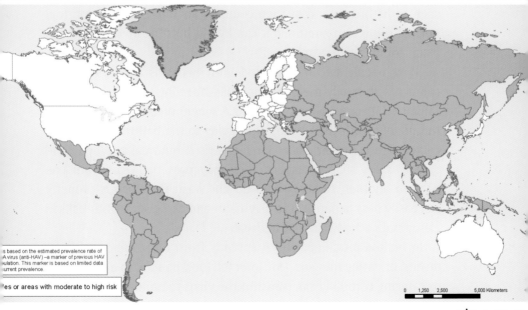

s based on the estimated prevalence rate of
A virus (anti-HAV) –a marker of previous HAV
ulation. This marker is based on limited data
urrent prevalence.

es or areas with moderate to high risk

0    1,250    2,500         5,000 Kilometers

s and names shown and the designations used on this map do not imply the expression of any opinion whatsoever
the World Health Organization concerning the legal status of any country, territory, city or area or of its authorities,
the delimitation of its frontiers or boundaries. Dotted lines on maps represent approximate border lines for which
yet be full agreement.

Data Source: World Health Organization/CDC
Map Production: Public Health Information
and Geographic Information Systems (GIS)
World Health Organization

**World Health Organization**

## Transmission of Hepatitis A

Hepatitis A is primarily passed via the oral-fecal route, which means that something we eat or drink has been contaminated by feces infected with the virus. Once ingested (taken in via food or drink), the hepatitis A virus passes through the stomach and into the intestines. From there, the virus enters the blood. The portal vein carries the infected blood from the intestines to the liver. Once in the liver, hepatitis A viruses invade the hepatocytes. The viruses start to churn out new viruses. Unlike most viruses, hepatitis A does not burst from the cell and destroy it. Instead, the hepatocytes expel the new "daughter viruses" into the bile. The bile is released into the stool, which then carries huge quantities of the virus out of the body. Those viruses can then infect the next unsuspecting person.

The hepatitis A virus is very hardy. It can live in water as hot as 140°F (60°C). The virus can also survive in temperatures below freezing (32°F, or 0°C). The hepatitis A virus can survive on surfaces such as bathroom and kitchen counters for more than a month at normal room temperatures. It can live in both freshwater and salt water for many months.

Most people become infected with hepatitis A through close contact with family members or while traveling to areas with poor sanitation. People can get hepatitis A when infected people do not thoroughly wash their hands after going to the bathroom. Day care centers are common places for hepatitis A outbreaks. When child care workers change diapers, they may pass the virus from one baby to another. Toddlers who do not wash their hands properly can easily pass hepatitis A to playmates and caregivers. Outbreaks in elementary schools are not unusual.

In restaurants, hepatitis A spreads from dirty hands to food, dishes, or eating utensils. One infected food handler in a restaurant or catering company can transmit the virus to hundreds of people.

www.usatoday.com

USA TODAY

Life
SECTION D

July 29, 2009

From the Pages of USA TODAY

# Beach pollution still nationwide problem

Raw sewage and other pollution continued to foul American beaches in 2008. For the fourth year in a row, more than 20,000 beach closing days were reported in the USA, according to a report released today by the Natural Resources Defense Council (NRDC) in Washington, D.C.

"Storm water and sewage runoff are the biggest sources for the contamination," says Nancy Stoner, NRDC's water program co-director. The report monitored beaches along the Atlantic, Pacific and Gulf coasts, along with those in the Great Lakes states.

The biggest factor that causes polluted beaches is rain, says Stoner. It carries pollutants from dirty storm water and overflowing sewage into streams and rivers, which eventually make their way to the ocean.

Beach water pollution, such as human or animal waste, makes swimmers vulnerable to a wide range of waterborne illnesses, including skin rashes, pinkeye, ear/nose/throat problems, dysentery, respiratory ailments, neurological disorders, hepatitis, and other serious health problems.

A tip from Stoner for your beach vacation this summer: "Don't swim after a heavy rainfall. Wait at least 24 hours."

—*Doyle Rice*

Food handlers are not always to blame, however. The food itself may be contaminated with hepatitis A long before it reaches the restaurant. For example, farmworkers with dirty hands can infect fresh produce. Contamination can occur during processing and distribution of food or during preparation at home or in restaurants. Lettuce, green onions, tomatoes, mixed salad greens, sandwiches, strawberries, and raspberries have all been linked to outbreaks of hepatitis A. All these foods are usually eaten without being cooked.

# Anatomy of a Hepatitis A Outbreak

In November 2003, disease detectives from the Centers for Disease Control and Prevention went to Pennsylvania to investigate an outbreak of hepatitis A. The sick people had all eaten at a restaurant in the small town of Monaca. More than 550 people from seven states came down with hepatitis A after eating at the restaurant.

At first, health officials believed the hepatitis originated with one of several food service workers who were sick with the disease. After interviewing restaurant staff, however, officials realized that the timing was not right. The food handlers had become ill at the same time as the customers.

The investigators then turned their attention to food served at the restaurant. CDC officials interviewed hundreds of people to determine which food all of them had eaten. As you can imagine, it's hard to remember what you ate a month ago! Ultimately, officials identified raw green onions as the source of the hepatitis A virus.

The onions were probably contaminated on Mexican farms during growing, harvesting, or packing. Infected people might have harvested or handled the onions. Water used in irrigation, rinsing, or icing down the produce could have carried the virus. At the restaurant, the cooks used the raw onions to make salsa. Had the onions been cooked, the heat would have killed the virus and the outbreak might have been avoided.

About nine thousand people who had eaten at the restaurant or been exposed to people involved in the outbreak received protective immunoglobulin injections. Three people died of hepatitis A infections related to this incident.

Many people contract hepatitis A by eating clams, oysters, mussels, and other shellfish that have lived in contaminated water. These creatures concentrate the virus in their bodies as they feed. One of the biggest outbreaks of hepatitis A occurred in 1988, when three hundred thousand people in Shanghai, China, ate clams harvested from a polluted river. Often people cook clams and mussels just until the shells open, which is not long enough to kill the virus. Other people eat raw oysters and are quickly infected if hepatitis A is present. People can also become infected by drinking contaminated water or by using ice cubes made from contaminated water.

While hepatitis A is not generally considered a sexually transmitted disease, it can be transmitted through sex. Although transmission via blood is not common, for a few days after infection, hepatitis A can be passed by blood transfusions or by sharing needles for injecting drugs.

*County health officials traced the hepatitis A outbreak in Ethan's hometown to an infected worker at the pizza restaurant. The employee sliced the meats and vegetables for the pizzas. While the man claimed that he always washed his hands thoroughly after going to the bathroom, more than seventy-five people who ate at the restaurant came down with hepatitis A. The newspaper reported that the man may have contracted hepatitis A from his girlfriend, who works at a day care center where two children were infected.*

## Course of the Disease

Regardless of how a person contracts the hepatitis A virus, the course of the disease is always the same. Unlike hepatitis B and C, which can cause chronic disease, hepatitis A causes only acute hepatitis. The period of illness and recovery is six months or less.

The incubation period, which is the length of time between the virus entering the body and the first onset of symptoms, averages about one month. The length of the incubation period is directly related to the level of infection: the higher the "dose" of viruses entering the body, the shorter the incubation period. People can pass the disease to others two weeks before and one week after the onset of symptoms. This is one reason it is so easy to develop hepatitis A: people can readily pass it on to others before realizing they are sick.

The younger people are, the less likely they are to have symptoms. In fact, 70 percent of children under the age of six with hepatitis A have no symptoms at all. They look normal and feel well. Parents do not realize their children are sick. Those infected children can pass hepatitis A on to their siblings, parents, grandparents, and the kids next door.

Most children aged seven and up, adolescents, and adults will develop symptoms with hepatitis A infection. Some will have nonspecific symptoms such as headaches, loss of appetite, abdominal pain, nausea, vomiting, and diarrhea. These people might think they have a cold, the flu, a stomach virus, or perhaps a mild case of food poisoning. They may stay home from work or school for a few days. They generally recover without any problems.

About 70 percent of people will suddenly develop jaundice. The symptoms of jaundice include yellowing of the sclera, dark urine, clay-colored stools, and severe itching. These symptoms generally send people to their doctors to find out what is wrong. The doctor may discover the liver is enlarged or tender. Hepatitis virus studies may show acute infection with hepatitis A. Symptoms can last one or two months. People usually start to feel better shortly after the onset of jaundice. The vast majority of people are completely well within six months.

However, hepatitis A can cause serious illness. Between 11 and 22 percent of adults with hepatitis A infection are sick enough to be hospitalized for their illness. Rarely, people infected with hepatitis A develop fulminant hepatitis, which leads to sudden liver failure within a few weeks. People with fulminant hepatitis are placed in intensive care units. Most will not recover without a liver transplant. About one hundred Americans die from fulminant hepatitis A each year. Hepatitis A can be very serious for older people. People over fifty years old are five to ten times more likely to die from hepatitis A than all other age groups combined.

Once people recover from hepatitis A, they are immune to it for the rest of their lives. Having immunity means they can never get hepatitis A again. During the course of the illness, the immune system forms protective antibodies against the virus. The liver clears the virus from the body and repairs any damage.

If someone has had hepatitis A in the past, blood tests will find hepatitis A antibodies. This is important information for doctors. For example, a doctor may want to see if a person has already had hepatitis A before administering the hepatitis A vaccine. People who had hepatitis A in the past are immune to it and do not require vaccination.

## Prevention of Hepatitis A

Basic good hygiene can go a long way toward preventing infection with hepatitis A. People should wash their hands for at least thirty seconds (as long as it takes to sing the "Happy Birthday" song twice) with plenty of soap and warm water, after going to the bathroom, changing diapers, playing with young children, and before preparing food. People who prepare food for others in restaurants should wear gloves. Many restaurants require employees to wear disposable plastic gloves while preparing food.

Proper hand washing requires thoroughly rinsing hands with running water after lathering with soap for twenty to thirty seconds.

To kill the hepatitis A virus, foods should be heated to at least 185°F (85°C) for one minute or more. Vigorously washing raw produce in tap water greatly reduces the risk of contracting hepatitis A. For example, washing lettuce reduces the number of viruses on the leaves by tenfold to one hundredfold. Cleaning kitchens and bathrooms with solutions of diluted bleach or ammonia and other common household cleaners also kills the virus.

## The Hepatitis A Vaccine

Hepatitis A is the most common vaccine-preventable disease in the world. The first hepatitis A vaccine became available in 1995. Originally, the FDA only approved the vaccine for children aged two and up. Because the vaccine proved so effective and was so safe, the FDA approved it for even younger children in 2005. There are two vaccines for hepatitis A. The first, HAVRIX, contains a preservative. The second, VAQTA, has no preservative. The viruses used in the vaccinations are inactive, so they cannot cause hepatitis.

The CDC and American Academy of Pediatrics, an association of doctors who treat children, recommend that all children receive a vaccination for hepatitis A at aged one. They receive the second shot in the two-part series six to twelve months later. Within four weeks of their first shot, 97 percent of children develop antibodies to the virus. One hundred percent have protective antibodies after their second dose. The vaccine works just as well for older children and adults who have not been immunized before. The vaccines provide protection against hepatitis A for twenty years or more.

In 2001 the FDA approved a combination vaccine called Twinrix for hepatitis A and B in people aged eighteen and older. Three injections are required for full immunity against both diseases.

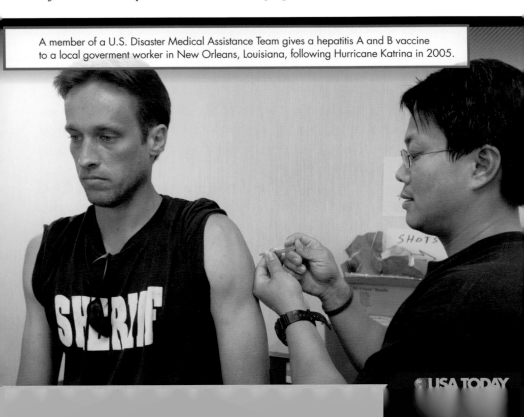

A member of a U.S. Disaster Medical Assistance Team gives a hepatitis A and B vaccine to a local goverment worker in New Orleans, Louisiana, following Hurricane Katrina in 2005.

USA TODAY

www.usatoday.com

USA TODAY

Life

SECTION D

**June 16, 2009**

From the Pages of USA TODAY

# For the most part, the kids are all right: Devoted parents keep children safer, healthier than ever before

Here's some welcome news for the parents of America: You're doing a great job.

Although exhausted moms and dads may not hear it often enough, research shows that their devotion is paying off. In dozens of important ways, kids are far healthier and safer today than they were even a generation ago. "Things are tremendously safer now for our children than they were for us, and they continue to improve each year," says pediatric trauma surgeon David Mooney, director of the trauma program at Children's Hospital Boston.

In the past century, the infant mortality rate has declined with each generation,

The CDC recommends the hepatitis A vaccination for U.S. citizens who are at risk of getting hepatitis A and for those who could become seriously ill if infected with the virus. The following groups are considered to be at risk:

- Travelers to all parts of the world except Australia, Canada, Japan, New Zealand, Scandinavia, Western Europe, and the United States
- Men who have sex with men
- People who share needles or syringes when they inject drugs
- People with certain blood-clotting problems
- People with job-related risks, such as doctors, nurses, paramedics, scientists who work with primates, and laboratory

falling from 29 deaths per 1,000 births in 1950 to 13 deaths per 1,000 births in 1980 to just under seven deaths per 1,000 births today, according to the Centers for Disease Control and Prevention. Babies are more likely to survive for many reasons, from cleaner water to vaccines, antibiotics, good prenatal care and better nutrition.

And kids of all ages are benefiting from a wealth of new research, as well as the safety laws and better products based on those research findings.

"Tens of thousands of children are alive today because of the effort that everybody has made, including loving parents," says Alan Korn, executive director of Safe Kids USA, a non-profit advocacy group.

**What parents do right**

Progress in key areas include vaccinating.

About 77% of children ages 19 to 35 months received all recommended vaccinations in 2007 and 90% were vaccinated against chickenpox.

Vaccines have nearly eliminated deaths from diphtheria, mumps, pertussis, tetanus, polio, measles and rubella, according to the CDC. Newer vaccines, approved since 1980, have reduced the number of deaths from hepatitis A, acute hepatitis B, Haemophilus influenzae, or Hib, and chicken pox, by 80% or more. And thanks to one of the newest vaccines, approved in 2000, deaths from invasive pneumococcal disease have fallen 25%.

"Giving vaccines is one of the most important ways that parents can keep their children safe," says infectious-disease expert Joseph Bocchini.

—Liz Szabo

workers who handle infected blood or stools
- People who have chronic liver disease, including hepatitis B, hepatitis C, or cirrhosis
- Anyone who has had or is waiting for a liver transplant

Another highly effective way to prevent hepatitis A infection is with immunoglobulin. This injectable medication contains concentrated human antibodies prepared from human blood. Immunoglobulin provides people with temporary antibodies to fight the hepatitis A virus until their own immune systems build up antibodies through vaccination. The protective effects of immunoglobulin last from three to five months.

When given within two weeks after exposure to hepatitis A, immunoglobulin is about 90 percent effective in preventing the disease. It also may lessen the severity of the disease. Immunoglobulin is useful in several situations: in babies who are too young to get the hepatitis A vaccine (under the age of one) and for people who must travel before they receive their second dose of the vaccine. Immunoglobulin helps to prevent hepatitis A during outbreaks in day care centers or among restaurant patrons. It can also protect members of a family in which someone has hepatitis A.

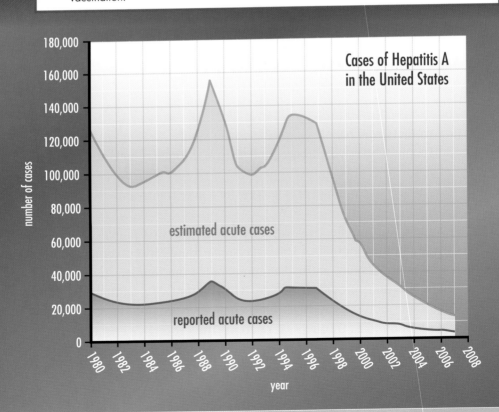

Cases of hepatitis A in the United States have been drastically reduced over time by vaccination.

Cases of Hepatitis A in the United States

number of cases

estimated acute cases

reported acute cases

year

*Ethan started to feel sick just a few days after he saw his doctor. He developed a mild fever and nausea and lost his appetite. After three weeks at home, Ethan returned to school. He still felt tired in the afternoons. After four months, Ethan felt as good as ever, and his doctor pronounced him cured. The hepatitis A vaccine didn't come into widespread use until Ethan was seven, so he had never been vaccinated. However, having hepatitis A one time made him immune to ever getting it again. Out of the six friends that Ethan ate with that night at the pizza parlor, three ended up with hepatitis A. All recovered without any complications or long-term damage to their livers.*

## Treatment of Hepatitis A

There is no specific treatment for hepatitis A. In most cases, doctors advise patients to stay home, get plenty of rest, drink fluids, and eat a healthy diet. Anyone infected with hepatitis A who has a fever should check with a doctor before taking medication. People should avoid all nonessential prescription and over-the-counter medications so that the liver can rest. People who normally drink alcohol should stop completely until their doctors say it is safe to resume moderate drinking. People with hepatitis A should be kind to their livers to help them recover more quickly.

People with hepatitis A should take steps to avoid infecting others. This includes common hygiene measures such as good hand-washing techniques. Infected people should not handle food or serve it to others. When people are no longer contagious, they may return to school and work, if they feel up to it and their doctor approves. It may be best to return to school or work part-time at first to avoid excessive fatigue. However, if people feel well, there is no medical reason why they cannot resume their normal activities.

# CHAPTER FOUR

# HEPATITIS B

**M**ai could hardly believe it. Her doctor said she has hepatitis B and that she could give it to her baby during delivery. The doctor explained that people usually become infected with hepatitis B in two ways: by sexual contact and at birth during the delivery process. Mai was born in China and adopted as a toddler by a U.S. couple. She learned that many people of Asian ancestry are infected at birth. People infected at birth are often unable to clear the virus from their bodies because babies have weak immune systems. Mai's doctor explained that most of those people still carry the virus. In many cases, these people never have any symptoms of their chronic hepatitis B.

Hepatitis B is one of the major diseases of humankind and is a serious global health concern. Currently, an estimated two billion people around the world are infected with hepatitis B. More than 350 million have chronic or lifelong infections. Hepatitis B causes an estimated 600,000 deaths each year, making it among the top ten causes of death worldwide. More than one-third of the world's people have been infected with hepatitis B during their lifetime. According to the CDC, about 1.25 million Americans are infected with hepatitis B. About 46,000 new infections occur annually,

Illustration of a hepatitis B virus

but only about 13,000 of those people become sick.

Hepatitis B is not even distantly related to the hepatitis A virus. Hepatitis B is the primary virus in a small group of viruses that make up the hepadnavirus family. Other viruses in this family are known to cause liver infections in mammals, such as woodchucks and ground squirrels, and in birds, such as ducks. However, only humans become infected with hepatitis B (although researchers have infected primates such as chimpanzees in experiments). The virus infects the liver, the kidneys, and the pancreas.

## Transmission of Hepatitis B

Hepatitis B is a dangerous virus. It is far easier to catch hepatitis B than HIV. In fact, the hepatitis B virus is fifty to one hundred times more contagious than HIV. Hepatitis B spreads by contact with bodily fluids and blood, just as HIV does. People can get hepatitis B in several ways. In the United States, about half of all new cases of hepatitis B are a result of sexual contact with an infected person. The virus has been found in semen, vaginal secretions, and saliva. This means that hepatitis B is transmissible between heterosexuals as well as same-sex couples of both genders. The risk of getting hepatitis B increases with the number of sexual partners a person has.

The virus can also spread through contact with blood or blood products. Prior to 1975, before blood banks tested for the virus, many people got hepatitis B after receiving donated blood or plasma. Hepatitis B can also spread when people share needles for injecting drugs. Sharing objects such as straws or dollar bills for snorting cocaine and other drugs may also spread hepatitis B, since people who use cocaine may have broken blood vessels inside their noses. Hepatitis B occasionally spreads through needles used for acupuncture, tattoos, and body piercing.

# Deadly Needles: What Do You Think?

In 2009 dozens of people in India died from hepatitis B because they were injected with "recycled" syringes and needles. Afterward, government investigators discovered warehouses filled with more than 300 tons (272 metric tons) of dirty syringes, needles, bags of partially used intravenous fluids, and medication vials. Women and children had been hired at low wages to sort through the medical waste. Once sorted, people repackaged the contaminated needles and syringes and sold them as new. The law requires the destruction of used medical supplies, but that was not done. A March 2009 study found that less than half of the hospitals, medical clinics, and doctors' offices in India were using the safe-injection practices recommended by the World Health Organization. By one estimate, every syringe in the country is reused an average of four times.

Over the past few years, an increasingly large number of Americans have traveled to India for medical care. In some cases, they go for cosmetic surgeries that would not be covered by insurance. These procedures are much cheaper in India than in the United States. The process of traveling abroad for medical care is so widespread that it has a name—medical tourism. Should people reconsider this practice? What do you think?

People can get hepatitis B by using personal items, such as razors or toothbrushes, that belong to an infected person. Young children who have hepatitis B can easily spread it by touching one another's cuts and scratches. Until a vaccine became available in 1982, health-care workers often got hepatitis B when they touched infected blood or accidentally stuck themselves with dirty needles.

An infected mother can pass hepatitis B to her newborn during childbirth. Often the mother does not know she has hepatitis B. This is the most common mode of transmission in many parts of the world. In the United States, all pregnant women are screened for hepatitis B before their babies are born. If the mother tests positive, her infant receives the hepatitis B vaccine within twelve hours of birth. Infected newborns will often receive hepatitis B immunoglobulin for additional protection as well. The hepatitis B virus can infect breast milk, so infected mothers should not breast-feed their babies.

The hepatitis B virus is robust. It can survive outside the body for at least seven days and still cause infection. This means that dried smears of infected blood on doorknobs, bathroom fixtures, and countertops are contagious. A solution made of one part household bleach and ten parts water will disinfect these surfaces. Anyone cleaning up blood or other body fluids, such as health-care workers or hospital housekeeping staff, should wear gloves for protection against accidental infection.

## Course of the Disease

Unlike hepatitis A, which causes only acute hepatitis, hepatitis B can cause either acute infection (lasting six months or less) or chronic infection (lasting more than six months). The incubation period for hepatitis B ranges from two to five months, with an average of three

**Sports**
SECTION C

**January 11, 2008**

From the Pages of USA TODAY

# Young athletes warned: Injections are serious subject

Roger Clemens' personal trainer did not inject him with steroids or human growth hormone, the seven-time Cy Young Award winner says. He insists the syringe needle that was plunged into his buttocks contained only B-12 vitamins and the numbing agent lidocaine.

To those fighting against the use of performance-enhancing drugs by high school athletes, Clemens' claim is both dubious and dangerous because of the risks involved with any injection.

"Young athletes are very impressed by what their sports heroes say and do," says Chuck Kimmel, president of the National Athletic Trainers' Association. "There's a real authority carryover in these situations. They assume because a person is an expert in one area that they're qualified in another."

months. During this time, people infected with hepatitis B usually feel well and do not know they are sick. It is easy for newly infected people to pass the hepatitis B virus to others during the incubation period.

Adults are much more likely than children to develop symptoms when they become infected with hepatitis B. About three out of ten people infected with hepatitis B do not have any symptoms. The seven out of ten people who do experience symptoms may develop jaundice, nausea, fatigue, loss of appetite, abdominal discomfort, and an altered sense of taste and smell.

The body mounts a vigorous attack against the hepatitis B virus. The immune system response causes symptoms such as inflammation of the blood vessels (called vasculitis) and inflammation of the

Kimmel says the injection of substances into the human body is fraught with serious consequences and should be done only by qualified medical personnel.

"ATCs (certified athletic trainers) are not licensed to give an injection," he says. Clemens' personal trainer, Brian McNamee, is not certified by the NATA.

According to the latest Youth Risk Behavior Surveillance survey of about 14,000 U.S. high school students, 4% said they had used steroids.

The danger is compounded by the practice of needle-sharing by young athletes.

The risk of blood-borne infections, such as hepatitis B, is so high that the British Association of Sport and Exercise Medicine has recommended that "adolescent athletes should be vaccinated against the virus as a routine."

Kimmel also says parents should be wary of their children receiving corticosteroid injections for joint inflammation. "The potential risk outweighs any potential gains and should be avoided at all costs." Parents should be proactive with their kids' coaches to make sure that risky behavior isn't tolerated.

"If a coach says your kid needs an injection, that should be a red flag," Kimmel says. "It all starts at home. Kids need to know that there are no shortcuts and no easy paths. Parents need to consult with the right people: their child's physician and a certified athletic trainer. Unfortunately, there are those people who are willing to risk their child's reputation and health. In the end, it's all about morals."

—Sal Ruibal

kidneys (glomerulonephritis). People may also develop rashes, fever, and abnormal protein in the urine. Up to 20 percent of people with an acute hepatitis B infection have severe pain and stiffness in their joints, similar to a person with arthritis.

As many as ninety-nine out of one hundred healthy adults with strong immune systems will completely eliminate the hepatitis B virus from their bodies within six months with no treatment. Less than 1 percent of adults will develop acute fulminant hepatitis B. As described earlier, people with acute fulminant hepatitis suffer sudden liver failure, with bleeding problems, encephalopathy, and coma. About 85 percent of people who have fulminant hepatitis B will die from liver failure, unless they receive a timely liver transplant.

USA TODAY

## Chronic Hepatitis B

When hepatitis B persists for longer than six months, doctors call it chronic hepatitis B. The risk of progressing from acute to chronic hepatitis B is age related. About 90 percent of infants infected at birth with hepatitis B develop chronic hepatitis B, while about 30 percent of children between the ages of one and five years develop it. People of any age who have HIV, have a compromised immune system due to an organ transplant, or are taking chemotherapy medications for cancer are far more likely to develop chronic hepatitis B. And for unknown reasons, men are six times more likely than women to develop chronic hepatitis B.

The gap between reported and estimated cases of hepatitis B in the United States has diminished in the last twenty years.

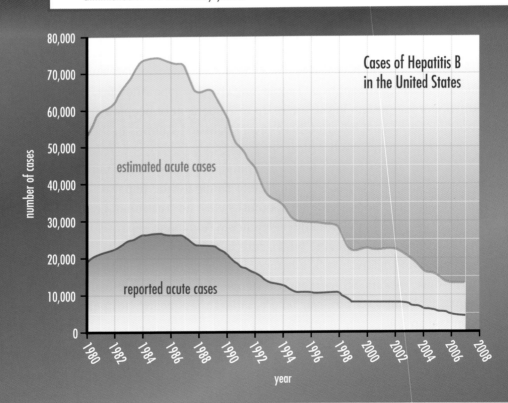

Cases of Hepatitis B in the United States

estimated acute cases

reported acute cases

number of cases

year

Why is being chronically infected with hepatitis B such a concern? People with chronic infection are often carriers of the virus and are able to infect others, sometimes for many years. They are more likely to develop liver damage, even if they initially feel well. About one-fourth of people chronically infected with hepatitis B die of cirrhosis or liver cancer.

Each year that people live with a chronic hepatitis B infection increases their chances of developing cirrhosis. Cirrhosis is a form of permanent liver damage. The liver becomes scarred and forms useless fibrotic tissue and nodules. The damaged liver looks and feels like a street paved with cobblestones. Infection overwhelms the plucky hepatocytes so they can no longer repair liver damage. In the United States, excessive alcohol intake is the most common cause of cirrhosis, with chronic hepatitis B and hepatitis C infections being the next most common causes. Advanced cirrhosis can lead to jaundice, weight loss, muscle wasting, kidney damage, encephalopathy (mental confusion), life-threatening bleeding, and death. An estimated five thousand Americans die each year from cirrhosis or liver cancer related to hepatitis B infection.

The risk of developing liver cancer is also increased among those with chronic hepatitis B infection. According to the CDC, hepatitis B is the cause of eight out of ten cases of liver cancer. Only tobacco causes more cancer than the hepatitis B virus. People with hepatitis B infection are one hundred times more likely to develop liver cancer than those without the infection. It takes twenty to thirty years to develop liver cancer due to hepatitis B infection, so people infected at birth would not be diagnosed until their twenties. Liver cancer often spreads to other organs, especially to the lungs. It is difficult to treat, and the chance of long-term survival is low.

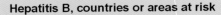

**Hepatitis B, countries or areas at risk**

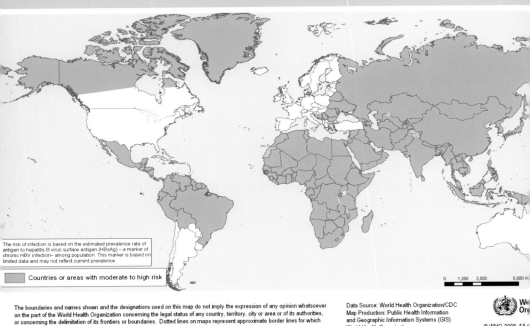

The risk of infection is based on the estimated prevalence rate of antigen to hepatitis B virus surface antigen (HBsAg) – a marker of chronic HBV infection– among population. This marker is based on limited data and may not reflect current prevalence.

Countries or areas with moderate to high risk

0      1,250    2,500              5,000 K

The boundaries and names shown and the designations used on this map do not imply the expression of any opinion whatsoever on the part of the World Health Organization concerning the legal status of any country, territory, city or area or of its authorities, or concerning the delimitation of its frontiers or boundaries. Dotted lines on maps represent approximate border lines for which there may not yet be full agreement.

Data Source: World Health Organization/CDC
Map Production: Public Health Information
and Geographic Information Systems (GIS)
World Health Organization

© WHO 2008. All

This map from the World Health Organization shows countries and areas at risk for hepatitis B.

## Prevention of Hepatitis B

Scientists developed the first hepatitis B vaccine in 1982. Since hepatitis B infection is the most common cause of liver cancer, a vaccine that prevents the infection also prevents the cancer. Overall, the vaccination is between 85 and 100 percent effective at preventing hepatitis B in people who receive the recommended three doses of vaccine. The immunity lasts for at least fifteen years.

The CDC and the American Academy of Pediatrics recommend that newborns get their first hepatitis B vaccination before they leave the hospital. They receive the second dose at one to two months of age and the third dose after the child turns two. A number of combination vaccinations provide immunity for diseases such as tetanus and diphtheria along with hepatitis A and B. The timing of these vaccinations varies from the recommended schedule for hepatitis B alone.

Adolescents and teens between the ages of eleven and nineteen who have never been vaccinated should be. Some states and school districts require children to be vaccinated for hepatitis B before they enter middle school if they were not vaccinated as infants. The younger people are when they are vaccinated, the more likely the vaccine will be completely effective.

## EFFECTIVENESS OF THE HEPATITIS B VACCINE BY AGE AND DOSE

| Vaccine Doses | Level of Effectiveness | |
| --- | --- | --- |
| | Children | Teens and Adults |
| 1 | 16% to 40% | 20% to 30% |
| 2 | 80% to 95% | 75% to 80% |
| 3 | 98% to 100% | 90% to 95% |

The highest rate of new hepatitis B infections in the United States occurs among adults between the ages of twenty and forty-nine. Yet one study showed that fewer than half of these people are being vaccinated. The people at increased risk of contracting hepatitis B include the following:

- Heterosexuals with multiple partners
- Men who have sex with men
- Infants born to infected mothers
- People who have been diagnosed with other sexually transmitted diseases, such as syphilis or gonorrhea
- People who inject illegal drugs
- Prison inmates
- Health-care workers (paramedics, doctors, nurses, dentists, laboratory staff)

- People who are on dialysis (receiving treatment to cleanse the blood when the kidneys have failed)
- Household and family members of infected people
- Immigrants and adopted children from countries where hepatitis B infection is common, including certain Asian nations (especially China) and the Pacific Islands

## Vaccine Side Effects

Serious side effects from hepatitis A and B vaccines are extremely rare. If side effects occur, they are generally mild. About half of the people who are vaccinated have a local reaction such as pain, redness, and swelling at the injection site. Cool wet cloths applied for ten minutes at a time every few hours can ease these symptoms. If the swelling persists longer than two days, people should contact their health-care providers for further advice.

Up to 20 percent of people may have a low fever, headache, or feel like they are coming down with the flu. This can happen with any vaccination. Babies less than six months old can be treated with the fever-reducing medication acetaminophen. With a doctor's permission, older babies can take either acetaminophen or ibuprofen. Children and adolescents can take acetaminophen or ibuprofen, unless their doctors say not to do so.

People under eighteen should never take aspirin or any product containing aspirin without the approval of a doctor. Aspirin use in this age group is associated with a rare but deadly condition called Reye's syndrome.

Unvaccinated people who have been exposed to hepatitis B will usually receive hepatitis B immunoglobulin to help protect them from developing an active infection. The first injection of the three-shot series of hepatitis B vaccination will often be given as well. While these people should get the complete series (over two years), even receiving one injection offers some protection.

People who have hepatitis B but have not had hepatitis A should receive the hepatitis A vaccine. Someone infected with both viruses is much more likely to suffer from an especially severe or even fatal illness than those who are infected with either virus alone. The hepatitis A vaccine is extremely effective at preventing the disease and may be lifesaving for someone also infected with hepatitis B.

In addition to vaccination, commonsense measures can help prevent infection with hepatitis B:

- Limit the number of sexual partners. The risk of infection increases with the number of partners.
- According to the CDC, the proper use of condoms might reduce transmission of hepatitis B, although it has not been conclusively proven to do so.
- People who use intravenous drugs should not share their equipment with anyone else.
- Tattoos and piercings should be done only at places with good safety records. Most states require tattoo and piercing parlors to be licensed.
- Health-care workers should wear protective eyewear and gloves whenever they touch blood and other bodily fluids.
- If a family member has hepatitis B, he or she must not share any personal care items, especially objects that might be contaminated with blood or other bodily fluids.

*While it is too late to protect Mai from hepatitis B, her baby will*

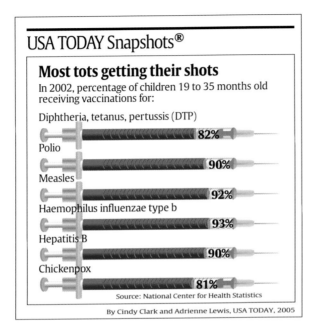

**USA TODAY Snapshots®**

**Most tots getting their shots**

In 2002, percentage of children 19 to 35 months old receiving vaccinations for:

Diphtheria, tetanus, pertussis (DTP)
82%

Polio
90%

Measles
92%

Haemophilus influenzae type b
93%

Hepatitis B
90%

Chickenpox
81%

Source: National Center for Health Statistics

By Cindy Clark and Adrienne Lewis, USA TODAY, 2005

receive the first dose of vaccine within twelve hours of birth. The baby will also receive an injection of immunoglobulin before leaving the hospital. The other two doses of the vaccine will be administered on schedule. This will protect Mai's baby from hepatitis B. "The doctor told me that I won't be able to breast-feed my baby," said Mai, "because that increases the risk of infection. That disappoints me, but I want to do what's best for my baby."

Thanks to prenatal testing and infant vaccination, the incidence of hepatitis B among children born in the United States has decreased greatly since the 1980s. U.S. public health officials encourage foreign-born residents, especially those born in Asian countries, to be tested for hepatitis B.

## Treatment of Hepatitis B

There is no particular treatment for acute hepatitis B infection. As with hepatitis A infection, people with acute hepatitis B should stay home from school or work if they don't feel well and should

## Hepatitis D

This strange little virus can only replicate in the presence of an active hepatitis B infection. About seventy thousand Americans infected with hepatitis B are also infected with hepatitis D. Having hepatitis D along with hepatitis B increases the risk of serious complications. Nearly one-fifth of patients with the D virus develop fulminant hepatitis, which is often deadly. Coinfection with the hepatitis B and D viruses kills about one thousand people in the United States each year. There is no vaccine to prevent hepatitis D, but being vaccinated against hepatitis B also prevents infection with the D virus.

get plenty of rest. They should stick to a healthy diet, drink plenty of fluids, and avoid alcohol entirely. People should check with their doctors before taking over-the-counter medications to be sure the medications will not interfere with the liver's recovery.

Most adults with acute hepatitis B recover fully and do not suffer any permanent liver damage. Recovery from acute hepatitis B infection is believed to give lifelong immunity to further infection by the virus, just as if the person had been vaccinated.

However, nine out of ten infants infected at birth and nearly one-half of children under the age of five are unable to clear the virus from their bodies because their immune systems are not strong enough. These children go on to develop chronic hepatitis B infection. Many of these children will grow up without even knowing they are infected. During those years, their livers are being quietly damaged, with scar tissue replacing healthy hepatocytes. Ultimately, cirrhosis or liver cancer develops among those infected at birth or in childhood. They may die in their thirties, forties, or fifties.

Patients with chronic hepatitis B must work closely with their doctors to decide when—or if—to begin medications for their infection. Patients who don't show signs of active infection or have little or no liver damage may not need medications. Treatment for hepatitis B is complex, time-consuming, and expensive, and carries the risk of significant side effects. Not every person with hepatitis B infection is a good candidate for treatment. Some people cannot be helped because their disease has advanced too far or because they carry a form of the virus that cannot be helped by treatment.

Scientists don't think it is possible to completely and permanently eliminate the virus from the body once a person is chronically infected. Instead, the treatment goal for hepatitis B is to slow or stop viral replication, to reduce liver inflammation, and to keep the disease from progressing to cirrhosis or liver cancer.

## MEDICAL TREATMENT

Scientists have made impressive advances in treatments for chronic hepatitis B in recent years. Medications used for the treatment of viral infections are called antiviral drugs. Because it can take many years for hepatitis B to damage the liver, it is not yet known if these antiviral medications actually prevent cirrhosis or liver cancer. The antiviral remedies used to treat hepatitis B are listed below. This list includes the year of FDA approval and brand name for each medication in parentheses.

Interferon alfa-2b (1992, Viraferon)
Lamivudine (1998, Epivir-HBV)
Adefovir (2002, Hepsera)
Entecavir (2005, Baraclude)

Telbivudine (2006, Tyzeka)
Tenofovir (2008, Viread)
Peginterferon alfa-2a (2005, Pegasys)

While these antiviral medications work in similar ways and have similar side effects, patients often respond better to one than to another. Having several effective antivirals to choose from allows doctors to individualize treatment plans for their patients. Some patients receive two or more of the medications at the same time.

Interferons are a group of proteins that the body makes in response to viral infections. They *interfere* with viral replication and protect noninfected cells against infection. Interferons may even reverse liver scarring. However, the body cannot always produce enough interferons to cure a chronic hepatitis B infection. Scientists have developed several synthetic (human-made) interferons. Injections of interferon alfa-2b are one treatment for hepatitis B. Interferon alfa-2b

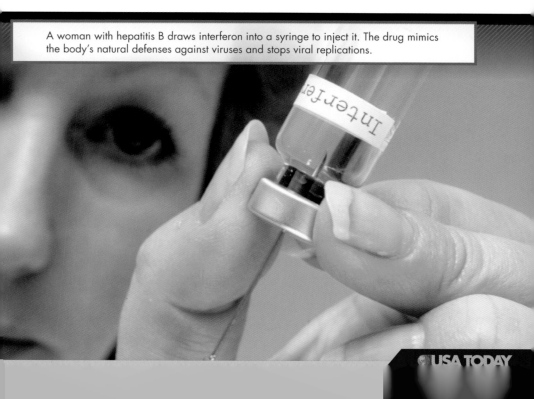

A woman with hepatitis B draws interferon into a syringe to inject it. The drug mimics the body's natural defenses against viruses and stops viral replications.

USA TODAY

www.usatoday.com

USA TODAY
**Life**
SECTION D

**January 23, 2006**

From the Pages of USA TODAY

# Hepatitis, 'the silent killer,' driven out of the shadows

There was a time when Arline Loh of Wilmington, Del., didn't tell people she has hepatitis B. "It carries such a stigma," says Loh, 57, an information technology expert who retired because of liver damage caused by the disease. "Hepatitis B is classified as an STD (sexually transmitted disease)."

It can be transmitted sexually, but Loh contracted the disease at birth from her mother, who carried the virus. About 90% of babies who are infected at birth develop chronic infection, compared with 6% of those infected later in life.

Until recent years, there was little the medical profession could do to help. Loh says the doctor who diagnosed her 17 years ago told her to "rest, and maybe you'll get better." That has changed. "Now there are drugs available to manage and treat this disease," says Loh.

Hepatitis B disproportionately affects Asians and Pacific Islanders, who account for over half of the more than 1.3 million carriers of the virus, says hepatitis researcher Samuel So, director of the Asian Liver Center at Stanford University School of Medicine. Hepatitis rates among Asian-Americans are higher because the rates are high in many of their countries of origin, according to the Asian Liver Center.

China, where Loh was born, bears the world's highest rate of hepatitis B, he says. About one in 10 are infected, and about half a million people there die each year. "We call it the silent killer," So

was widely used until 2005, when a longer-acting form of interferon, peginterferon alfa-2a, became available.

Lamivudine is an antiviral medication that was first used to treat people with AIDS. About 10 percent of HIV-infected people are also infected with chronic hepatitis B. When AIDS patients took lamivudine, doctors noticed that it seemed to slow replication of the hepatitis B says. "Many people who are infected don't know it because they feel perfectly healthy."

Studies show that 10% to 20% of Asian-Americans have chronic hepatitis B infection. And carriers with no symptoms can unwittingly pass it on to their sexual partners or to their children.

Vaccination has helped reduce the rate of hepatitis B from an average of 260,000 new cases a year in the 1980s, when the vaccine was licensed, to about 73,000 in 2003 according to the Centers for Disease Control and Prevention.

—*Anita Manning*

Arline Loh is working to promote awareness of hepatitis B. She holds some of the many medications she takes to treat her hepatitis and related illnesses.

virus as well. Doctors began to give lamivudine to people infected with hepatitis B alone. Patients take either a tablet or liquid once daily by mouth. Side effects are uncommon but can include headache, diarrhea, fatigue, nausea, abdominal pain, muscle aches, and rashes.

Lamivudine is effective at slowing viral replication and reducing liver inflammation and scarring. A major problem with lamivudine is that the virus often becomes resistant to the drug over time. This means that the medication is no longer effective or is less effective against the virus. In about two-thirds of people who receive lamivudine, the hepatitis B virus becomes resistant to the medication within four years. Also, when the medication is stopped, many of the people treated with it experience a sudden worsening of their hepatitis. Still, until resistance develops, it is very useful at postponing liver damage.

Adefovir is also used to treat both HIV infection and chronic hepatitis B. It comes in a tablet taken once daily by mouth. Adefovir's major side effect is kidney damage. This can occur when the medication is given at the higher dose required to treat HIV. It happens less often when taken for hepatitis B. Minor side effects include headache, diarrhea, weakness, and abdominal pain. Adefovir is effective at slowing viral replication and reducing liver damage. Doctors may use adefovir when patients become resistant to lamivudine. However, as with lamivudine, patients tend to have a recurrence of their hepatitis if adefovir is stopped. Some doctors think that treatment with adefovir has to continue for life.

Entecavir comes in tablet or liquid form and is taken once daily. Side effects are similar to those of the other oral antiviral medications, including headaches, abdominal pain, diarrhea, fatigue, and dizziness. Patients on entecavir show much less liver inflammation and scarring than those on lamivudine. The medication does not appear to cause resistance in the hepatitis B virus as lamivudine does. Many doctors prescribe entecavir instead of lamivudine and adefovir.

Telbivudine is very effective at both reducing the amount of hepatitis B virus in the liver and reducing inflammation of the liver itself. The most common side effects are muscle weakness, muscle pain, upper respiratory infection, cough, fatigue, headache, and abdominal pain.

Tenofovir slows the hepatitis B virus by blocking an enzyme needed for replication. Patients take one tablet daily. The most common side effect is nausea. In rare cases, kidney damage and bone thinning can occur.

Peginterferon alfa-2a is a human-made interferon. Peginterferon is longer acting than interferon and is injected just once a week instead of three times a week, like earlier forms of interferon. The drug is released gradually into the body. This continuous high level of medication seems to produce a better response in patients when given for several months to a year.

People taking peginterferon (or any form of interferon) are likely to experience moderate to serious side effects. Some people feel so sick they miss days, weeks, or even months of work. Common side effects include fever, chills, headache, muscle and joint aches, generalized weakness, and fatigue. Other symptoms include depression, loss of appetite, and nausea.

Some people on peginterferon experience fewer side effects after the first month or two of treatment. Others do better if the doctor reduces the dose. A few lucky people experience hardly any symptoms and can keep up their normal daily activities. Once the peginterferon treatment is over, most people feel it was worth living through all the side effects. Treatment generally lasts for sixteen to forty-eight weeks.

## LIVER TRANSPLANT

Each year at least 5,000 Americans die of cirrhosis or liver cancer caused by hepatitis B infection. Liver transplantation could be a lifesaving therapy for some of those people, but only 200 to 250 hepatitis B patients receive new livers each year. Some of those patients are not medically eligible for a transplant because they are too ill or have other health conditions that make a successful liver transplant

## USA TODAY Snapshots®

### Organ donations give life

In 1954, the kidney was the first human organ to be transplanted successfully. Today there are many kinds of transplants, including heart, liver and lungs.

How many people receive an organ transplant each day: **70**

How many people die each day because of a shortage of organs: **16**

Candidates on waiting list as of Feb. 2: **87,306**

Sources: United Network for Organ Sharing, Department of Health and Human Services

By Shannon Reilly and Dave Merrill, USA TODAY, 2005

unlikely. Many people who qualify for a transplant cannot receive one because of the shortage of available livers.

Many hepatitis B patients who receive new livers suffer a surge of infection because of the antirejection medications they must take after the transplant. Antirejection medications suppress the body's immune system, so that the body will not

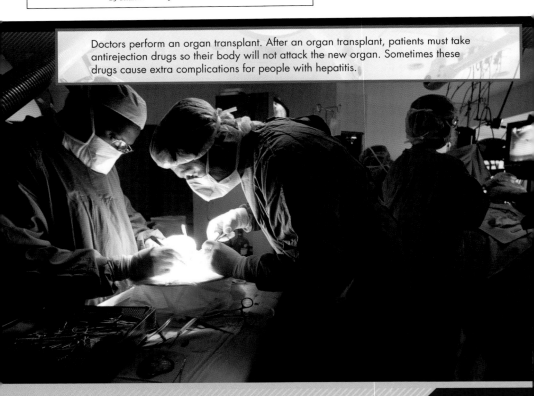

Doctors perform an organ transplant. After an organ transplant, patients must take antirejection drugs so their body will not attack the new organ. Sometimes these drugs cause extra complications for people with hepatitis.

reject the new liver. That's good for the liver, but it means the body cannot fight off infections very well.

Scientists are not certain that liver transplants totally eliminate hepatitis B from the body. However, new advances in post-transplant therapy offer promise. Antiviral medications given after a transplant decrease the chance of a flare-up of the disease. Some patients may need lifelong antiviral therapy. Adding hepatitis B immunoglobulin after transplant appears to further increase the probability of success.

*Mai's husband tested positive for infection with hepatitis B. Mai had no idea that she had infected her husband. She felt terrible about it. But his blood tests showed that he had recovered from an acute infection some time ago. Unlike Mai, he did not go on to develop chronic hepatitis B. Mai and her husband plan to see a liver specialist after their baby is born. Because she is young and otherwise healthy, Mai wants to talk to the specialist about beginning treatment for her hepatitis B. Early treatment can prevent the development of cirrhosis and liver cancer for some patients. Mai has little or no permanent damage to her liver, so she may decide to postpone treatment until her baby is older.*

# CHAPTER FIVE

# HEPATITIS C

*t's been ten years since Charlie learned that he had been infected with hepatitis C through a blood transfusion. His doctor detected the beginning of liver damage. She recommended that Charlie undergo treatment with the antiviral medication ribavirin and the long-acting form of interferon called peginterferon. Charlie and his wife met with the doctor to discuss treatment. The doctor showed Charlie's wife how to give the injection of peginterferon that he will need to take each week for forty-eight weeks. They discussed the side effects of treatment and the fact that Charlie might need to take time off work. He is a teacher and wants to begin treatment once school ends for the summer. But the doctor feels the treatment needs to start right away, even though it's the middle of the school year.*

Hepatitis C was originally called non-A, non-B hepatitis. Although people with the infection clearly had hepatitis, the virus could not be identified as either A or B. It was also known as post-transfusion hepatitis because it occurred most often after blood transfusions in the years before health-care workers could screen blood for the virus. In 1989 researchers identified the virus and renamed it hepatitis C.

According to the CDC, an estimated 3.2 million Americans are infected with hepatitis C. This makes hepatitis C the most widespread bloodborne infection in the United States. About nineteen thousand Americans become newly infected with hepatitis C each year. Worldwide, about 170 million people, or 3 percent of the global population, may be infected with hepatitis C. Only a small portion of those people know they are infected.

The hepatitis C virus is very different from the hepatitis A and B viruses. Hepatitis C is a member of the family of flaviviruses. The virus known as West Nile virus is a flavivirus, as are the viruses that cause yellow fever, dengue fever, and Saint Louis encephalitis. Unlike those viruses, however, hepatitis C cannot be passed by the bite of an infected mosquito. Hepatitis C infects only humans and chimpanzees. While hepatitis C infects primarily the liver, the virus can also be found outside the liver.

There are at least six different genotypes, or genetically distinct variations, of hepatitis C virus. Within the genotypes are at least fifty subtypes, which are identified by letters. It's sort of like a big family made up of siblings, half siblings, first cousins, and cousins once removed. They are all related, but each is genetically unique.

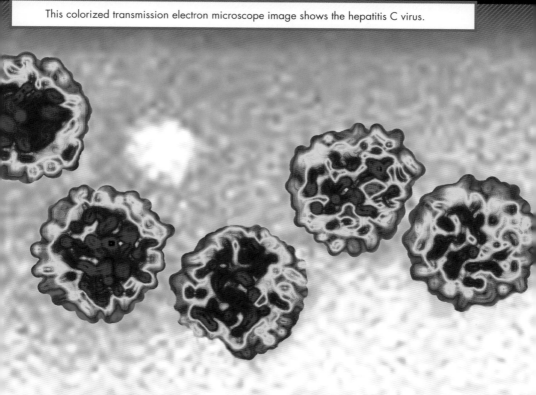

This colorized transmission electron microscope image shows the hepatitis C virus.

USA TODAY

In the United States, about three-fourths of hepatitis C infections are caused by genotypes 1a and 1b, which are more resistant to treatment than the other genotypes. Infection with one genotype or subtype of hepatitis C does not protect against future infection with another type.

## Transmission of Hepatitis C

Hepatitis C primarily spreads by contact with infected blood. Before scientists devised tests to detect the virus in donated blood, receiving a blood transfusion was the most common way to become infected with hepatitis C. The CDC estimates that about three hundred thousand Americans were infected with hepatitis C via blood or blood products prior to 1990. Blood products include packed red blood cells, platelets, fresh frozen plasma, and immunoglobulin.

Since 1990, screening donated blood for hepatitis C has been very effective. In the twenty-first century, the risk of getting hepatitis C from donated blood is very small—about one in two million units of transfused blood are contaminated with hepatitis C. However, if someone is newly infected when he or she donates blood, screening tests might not detect the virus.

About seven out of every ten new cases of hepatitis C in the United States occur among intravenous drug users who share contaminated needles. The longer a person uses injectable drugs, the greater the risk of being infected with hepatitis C. By some estimates, between 70 and 90 percent of long-term intravenous drug users carry the hepatitis C virus. People also can get hepatitis C by sharing straws or rolled-up dollar bills while snorting cocaine. Inserting such objects into the nose can break tiny blood vessels. Even a microscopic amount of infected blood is enough to carry the virus. In fact, hepatitis C is six times more contagious than HIV.

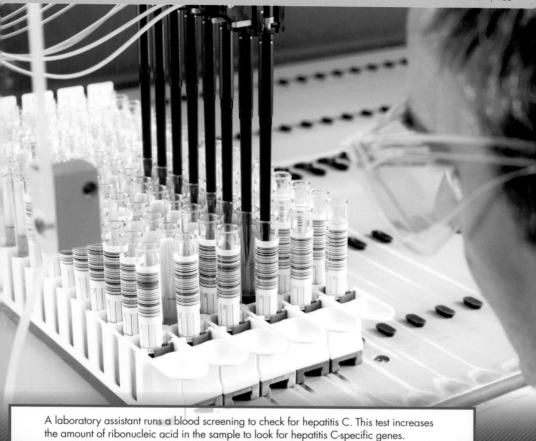

A laboratory assistant runs a blood screening to check for hepatitis C. This test increases the amount of ribonucleic acid in the sample to look for hepatitis C-specific genes.

Hepatitis C can be passed by other activities that involve contact with infected blood:

- Health-care workers can develop hepatitis C if stuck with infected needles or contaminated medical instruments. They can also become infected if contaminated blood splashes into their eyes, mouth, or open sore. There is a 2 to 3 percent chance of health-care workers developing hepatitis C after such an incident.
- The World Health Organization estimates that between 2.3 million and 4.7 million new cases of hepatitis C occur each year in poor countries. Doctors in poor countries often

reuse contaminated needles and medical equipment. A health worker might use a single needle and syringe to vaccinate dozens of children. In the United States and other wealthy nations, needles and syringes are used once and discarded.

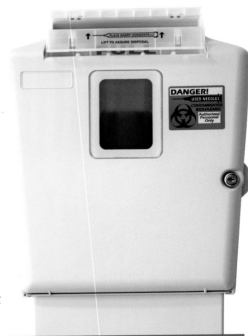

- Up to 30 percent of patients who receive hemodialysis (a treatment used to cleanse the blood when the kidneys fail) have hepatitis C. They got the virus from blood transfusions in the past. Other dialysis patients get hepatitis C because the shared dialysis equipment may not be properly sterilized. In 2009 the CDC reported that nine dialysis patients in New York City became infected from poorly cleaned equipment. The Department of Health ordered the dialysis center to pay large fines and permanently shut it down.

Hospitals, doctors offices, and other public facilities use special containers like this one to dispose of needles and syringes. This reduces the risk of people being exposed to bloodborne illnesses such as hepatitis.

- Family and others who are close to people with hepatitis C may become infected by sharing personal grooming items.
- Tattooing and body piercing equipment that is improperly sterilized can carry the virus.

# National Hepatitis C Prevention Strategy

The CDC developed a National Hepatitis C Prevention Strategy to protect public health. Goals of the plan include the following:

- Educating health-care workers and public health professionals so they can better identify and test people at risk for hepatitis C
- Educating the public about how to avoid becoming infected by hepatitis C and how to avoid passing it to others
- Monitoring acute and chronic disease trends
- Evaluating the effectiveness of prevention and treatment activities
- Ensuring that people with hepatitis C receive counseling and treatment
- Increasing research to better prevent and treat hepatitis C infection

- About 3 to 7 percent of infants of mothers infected with hepatitis C become infected during childbirth.
- Rarely, hepatitis C can be transmitted during sex. Hepatitis C has not been found in semen or saliva. But researchers believe that it can spread during sex only through breaks in the skin.

The hepatitis C virus can survive outside the human body and remain infectious for up to four days. This means that dried blood on personal care items and other surfaces is contagious during that time and may lead to hepatitis C infection. A solution of one part

USA TODAY

bleach and ten parts water is an effective disinfectant for these items. People who might have contact with blood or other body fluids, such as health-care workers and hospital cleaning staff, should wear gloves for protection against accidental infection.

## Course of the Disease

The incubation period for hepatitis C ranges from two weeks to five months, with an average of six to eight weeks. During those weeks, a person newly infected with hepatitis C probably feels well and is unaware of the infection. If an infected person donates blood or an organ during that time, the risk of transmitting the virus is great.

Like hepatitis B, hepatitis C may cause either acute infection (lasting fewer than six months) or chronic infection (lasting longer than six months). Between 15 and 25 percent of people infected with hepatitis C develop acute hepatitis and recover within six months. Many of these people have no symptoms. Their immune systems fight off the virus with little difficulty.

The symptoms of acute hepatitis C are mild and may be mistaken for the flu, as may happen with acute hepatitis A and B. These symptoms can include fatigue, loss of appetite, and weakness. Some people also develop muscle and joint aches, a skin rash, or jaundice. Oddly enough, people with the worst symptoms are also the ones most likely to completely clear the hepatitis C virus from their bodies and experience a full recovery. An increase in immune system activity results in an increase in symptoms. So more severe symptoms may mean that the body is actively fighting the virus.

The majority of people who develop acute hepatitis C, however, do not recover. Between 75 and 85 percent of people infected with hepatitis C develop the chronic form of the disease. When the human immune system attacks the hepatitis A or B viruses, there is a good chance the body can rid itself of infection. However, the immune system is not as successful when the enemy is hepatitis C.

Once established in the body, hepatitis C mutates, or changes, continually in an effort to trick the immune system. The mutations are often stronger than the initial virus. Doctors say people with hepatitis C are infected by different, closely related, but not identical, viruses. That is why so many people with the disease progress from acute to chronic infection.

Very few people with chronic hepatitis C know they have it because most have no symptoms. They may have injected drugs just once during their youth or received contaminated blood in a transfusion in the years before blood could be tested for hepatitis C. They may have become infected during military service by helping out a wounded buddy who was bleeding. Health-care workers can unknowingly contract hepatitis C while working in an emergency room or operating room.

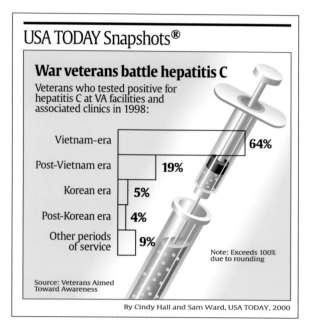

USA TODAY Snapshots®

**War veterans battle hepatitis C**

Veterans who tested positive for hepatitis C at VA facilities and associated clinics in 1998:

| | |
|---|---|
| Vietnam-era | 64% |
| Post-Vietnam era | 19% |
| Korean era | 5% |
| Post-Korean era | 4% |
| Other periods of service | 9% |

Note: Exceeds 100% due to rounding

Source: Veterans Aimed Toward Awareness

By Cindy Hall and Sam Ward, USA TODAY, 2000

The people most likely to be newly diagnosed with chronic hepatitis C are people born between 1945 and 1965. The majority of these people were likely infected during the 1970s and 1980s. Many of them have felt fine for twenty or more years. The number of newly diagnosed cases of chronic hepatitis C is expected to increase over the

> ## According to the CDC, of every 100 persons infected with hepatitis C . . .
>
> 75 to 85 will develop chronic infection
>
> 60 to 70 will develop chronic liver disease
>
> 5 to 20 will develop cirrhosis over twenty to thirty years
>
> 1 to 5 will die of liver cancer or cirrhosis

next ten years. This increase will be a result of the aging population seeking medical care for reasons that may be unrelated to hepatitis. For example, during an annual physical examination, a doctor may discover through a blood test that the patient also has hepatitis.

The hepatitis C virus thrives and replicates not just in the liver but in other parts of the body. The virus affects the stomach, lymph glands, bone marrow, and brain. In an infected person, the immune system is in a constant state of warfare with the hepatitis C virus. These symptoms can include the following:

- Skin disorders: There may be blisters on the hands, arms, and face; raised itchy areas in the mouth and nails and on the scalp; the extreme itching of pruritus; and the loss of pigment in the skin, known as vitiligo.
- Blood disorders: A liver infected with hepatitis C may be unable to produce the important proteins that regulate the clotting of blood. Blood vessels can become inflamed and may leak blood into the skin, especially in the legs. Bleeding into the kidneys and brain may occur. Red blood cells may be destroyed, resulting in anemia. Platelets, which help blood to

clot, may be lower than normal, which further increases the risk of bleeding.

- Autoimmune disorders: An unbalanced immune system might begin to attack the body, resulting in too many or too few thyroid hormones. Thyroid imbalance affects the entire body. If thyroid levels are too high, the body's metabolic rate speeds up. If thyroid levels are too low, the body slows down.
- Diabetes: A disorder of the pancreas gland that leads to too much sugar in the blood, diabetes occurs more commonly among those with hepatitis C infection. The virus may worsen diabetes among people who already have it.
- Kidney disorders: Hepatitis C infection may lead to kidney inflammation, a condition called glomerulonephritis. It results in blood and excess protein in the urine.

Some people with chronic hepatitis C will live for many years with few or no symptoms. As many as five out of twenty people with hepatitis C will develop cirrhosis over the course of twenty to thirty years. Cirrhosis can lead to blood–clotting problems; kidney disease; ascites; and portal hypertension, a dangerous condition that may cause life-threatening bleeding into the stomach and esophagus. A damaged liver might also lead to the buildup of ammonia in the body. This may cause encephalopathy, a disease of the brain marked by confusion, personality changes, and an inability to concentrate. It can progress to coma and death.

Anyone with cirrhosis is at high risk for liver cancer. People with hepatitis C are twenty-five times more likely to develop liver cancer than are people without the infection. It takes approximately thirty years from the time of the initial infection with hepatitis C for liver cancer to develop. Although hepatitis B is the most common cause of liver cancer in the United States, hepatitis C is a major cause as well.

www.usatoday.com

USA TODAY

Life

SECTION D

**MAY 9, 2007**

From the Pages of USA TODAY

# Hepatitis C may boost risk for non-Hodgkin's lymphoma

### Study could bolster infection's link to cancer

People infected with the hepatitis C virus may be at increased risk for a cancer called non-Hodgkin's lymphoma, according to a study in the *Journal of the American Medical Association*.

Doctors have long known that the virus causes chronic hepatitis, a liver inflammation, as well as cirrhosis and liver cancer. The new analysis is one of the largest, however, to find a relationship between hepatitis C and lymphoma, according to John Niederhuber, director of the National Cancer Institute, which helped finance the study.

Doctors reviewed the records of patients in the Department of Veterans Affairs medical system, including 146,000 with hepatitis C and 572,000 who were uninfected. After more than five years of follow-up, patients with hepatitis C were 20% to 30% more likely to develop non-Hodgkin's lymphoma, which develops in immune cells called lymphocytes.

Doctors can reduce the risk of cancer and other diseases by treating hepatitis C with antiviral medications. Worldwide, about one in five cancers are caused by infection. Doctors can prevent some of these cancers with vaccines, such as the hepatitis B vaccine, which can reduce the risk of liver cancer, or the vaccine against human papillomavirus, which protects against most cervical cancers.

—*Lisa Szabo*

Worldwide, liver cancer is the fifth most common cancer in men and the ninth most common in women. Hepatitis C kills approximately eight thousand to ten thousand Americans each year. That number is expected to increase over the next two decades as infected people begin to develop cirrhosis and liver cancer.

# Prevention of Hepatitis C

With its six genotypes and a dozen or more subtypes, the hepatitis C virus is a master of disguise. Scientists have not developed a vaccine to prevent hepatitis C because a vaccine that prevents one genotype or subtype does not prevent the others. In addition, the virus frequently mutates. It takes only one small change in the genetic makeup of a virus to make a vaccine for it useless.

Scientists continue to work on vaccines to prevent hepatitis C, but it is not likely that one will become available for several years. However, people with hepatitis C should be vaccinated against hepatitis A and hepatitis B. If someone infected with hepatitis C gets hepatitis A or B, he or she could become very ill and suffer a rapid worsening of the disease. The vaccines can protect the liver against additional damage.

In the absence of a vaccine to prevent hepatitis C, people can take specific steps to protect themselves against the disease:

- Do not use intravenous drugs. Anyone using drugs should stop and get into a treatment program. Those who cannot stop must never share needles, syringes, or other equipment. Almost every state and many communities offer free needle exchange programs that provide clean needles to drug users.
- Do not share personal grooming items that might have blood on them.
- Do not use cocaine. People who are unable to quit cocaine use should not share straws or rolled-up dollar bills for snorting the drug.
- Use care in choosing a body piercing or tattoo vendor.
- Even though hepatitis C seldom spreads by sexual contact, consistent condom use may decrease the risk, especially among those with multiple partners. Someone with hepatitis C should talk to a doctor about preventing transmission to sexual partners.

- Health-care workers should always follow routine safety precautions to prevent being stuck with infected needles or coming into contact with infected blood.

## Treatment of Hepatitis C

Chronic hepatitis C does not go away on its own. In most people, hepatitis C infection is a silent disease that progresses slowly over many years. A few people with chronic hepatitis C live long and healthy lives without the need for treatment. However, many others require medication or liver transplants to improve their quality of life or to save their lives. Medications for chronic hepatitis C can slow down viral replication, prevent further damage to the liver, decrease the risk for cirrhosis and liver cancer, and reduce current symptoms.

Some people with chronic hepatitis C are not treated, either

## Needle Exchange: What Do You Think?

Nearly every state offers needle exchange programs. Intravenous drug users turn in dirty needles and syringes and receive clean ones. Public health officials say this is a good idea because it slows the spread of diseases such as hepatitis C and HIV/AIDS, both of which are passed by contaminated blood. But some people believe that if it is easy for drug users to get clean needles, more people will turn to using illegal intravenous drugs. What do you think?

because they do not need treatment or because they have other health conditions that prevent treatment. People with chronic hepatitis C infection who are not being treated should see a doctor at least twice a year. Routine physical examinations and blood tests are the only way to monitor the disease. New research may one day provide treatments for every patient infected with hepatitis C. Until then, seeing a doctor is the best way to keep up with new developments.

## MEDICAL TREATMENT

The standard treatment for chronic hepatitis C is peginterferon plus the antiviral medication ribavirin. Interferons are a group of disease-fighting proteins made by the body in response to viral infections. Because the body cannot manufacture enough interferon on its own to win the war against hepatitis C, scientists developed synthetic forms of interferon.

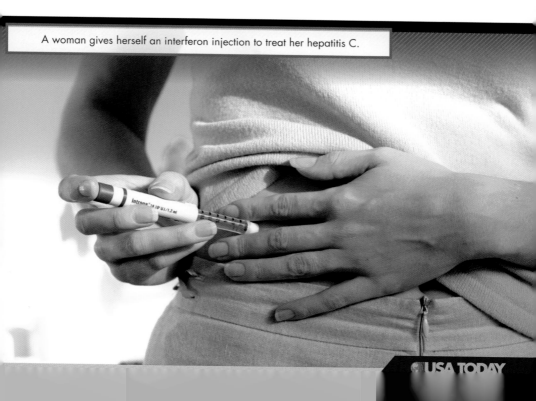

A woman gives herself an interferon injection to treat her hepatitis C.

USA TODAY

Peginterferon is a long-acting form of interferon that requires a once-weekly injection. Doctors use two forms of peginterferon: peginterferon alfa-2a (Pegasys) and peginterferon alfa-2b (Pegintron). All patients receive the same dosage of peginterferon alfa-2a, regardless of body weight. An individual's body weight determines the dosage of peginterferon alfa-2b. The medications are similar in safety and effectiveness.

*Charlie took peginterferon and ribavirin for forty-eight weeks. He had a tough time with his treatment. Fatigue was one of the worst problems for Charlie. "Some days I couldn't even walk up the stairs to my bedroom. For months, I slept downstairs on the living room couch," he recalls. "I lost 35 pounds [15.9 kg] because I could barely eat. Even though I cut back to three days a week at work, I could hardly make it in some days. My wife injected me on Friday evenings. I stayed in bed all weekend and most Mondays and Tuesdays. Some weeks I could only work Thursday and Friday. Then it was Friday night and time to start all over again."*

Patients take a combination of peginterferon and ribavirin for either twenty-four or forty-eight weeks. The antiviral medication Ribavirin works against a number of viruses. Patients take it by mouth twice a day during the treatment period. By itself, ribavirin has little effect on the hepatitis C virus. However, adding it to peginterferon doubles or triples the patient's chance of a sustained response, which means that the hepatitis C virus cannot be detected in the patient's blood for at least six months after treatment.

Patients infected with genotype 1 hepatitis C (the most common genotype in the United States) require treatment with combination therapy (peginterferon and ribavirin) for forty-eight weeks. About 40 to 45 percent of patients who get this treatment have a sustained response. However, patients infected with genotype 2 or genotype 3 hepatitis C have a much better outcome. They need only twenty-four weeks of combination therapy and experience a sustained response of 70 to 80 percent. A doctor will test the patient for the hepatitis C genotype before starting treatment. This test allows the patient to know what outcome to expect.

At least 10 percent of people undergoing treatment with peginterferon will experience moderate to severe side effects. The side effects are worse during the first few weeks of therapy, especially the days following the first injections. Adding ribavirin to the treatment makes some symptoms worse. People may have all or some of the following symptoms:

- Severe fatigue
- Muscle aches
- Headaches
- Nausea and vomiting
- Skin irritation at the injection site (for peginterferon)
- Weight loss
- Low-grade fever
- Irritability
- Depression
- Decreased numbers of red blood cells, white blood cells, and platelets
- Hair loss (usually returns after treatment is completed)
- Anemia
- Skin rash and itching
- Nasal stuffiness and inflamed sinuses
- Cough

Less common side effects may include thyroid disease, serious bacterial infections, seizures, ringing in the ears, and hearing loss.

www.usatoday.com
USA TODAY
**Life**
SECTION D

**October 19, 1999**

From the Pages of USA TODAY

# Hepatitis C behind bars: problem and solution

Public-health experts estimate that 20% to 60% of the 2 million people locked up on any given day are infected with the liver damaging virus hepatitis C. Infected people who leave prison can and will pass this virus to others.

Prison officials are starting to offer treatment for HIV infection, tuberculosis and other diseases but in most cases have balked at the high cost of treating prisoners with hepatitis C, says Jackie Walker of the National Prison Project of the American Civil Liberties Union in Washington, D.C.

In addition to the public health threat, non-treatment can turn even a short prison sentence into a death sentence. Walker says prisons are obligated to provide such lifesaving treatment to prisoners.

## TREATMENT WORKS FOR PRISONERS

Between 12% and 31% of the two million inmates in U.S. prisons are infected with chronic hepatitis C. Treating all prisoners who have hepatitis C with the standard therapy of peginterferon and ribavirin would be cost-effective. Treatment improves the quality of life and decreases long-term costs. Treatment should be coupled with educational and substance abuse programs. This significant proportion of infected individuals should not be denied access to therapy. "

—Jennifer A. Tan, Tom A. Joseph, and Sammy Saab, in Hepatology, 2008

In one study of Texas inmates, nearly 30% had hepatitis C. A similar study of California inmates found that 41% had hepatitis C infection.

But one of the formidable obstacles to curbing the disease is cost. "It's a very expensive disease to treat," says Edward Harrison, president of the National Commission on Correctional Health Care in Chicago, a group with a mission to improve the quality of the health care in U.S. prisons. Further, not everyone benefits from the two main drugs used to combat the virus, interferon and ribavirin.

Although prison officials are beginning to realize the scope of the problem, few states seem willing to fund treatment that could run into billions. At least one study projects the need for liver transplants because of hepatitis C will triple during the coming decade. At $250,000 a pop, that's a price tag no one wants to shoulder.

Although the rates of new hepatitis C infections have gone down, the high rates of the virus in prison represent a disease reservoir, one that could spill over its banks. "This is a major public health threat," says Jonathan Fielding, hepatitis C expert at the University of California.

—Kathleen Fackelmann

Rare side effects are heart and kidney failure, loss of vision, pneumonia, and septicemia (bacteria in the blood). Side effects and complications of treatment often disappear once the medications have been stopped. For most people, the potential for improvement and the lower risk of developing cirrhosis and liver cancer outweigh the side effects of hepatitis C treatment.

People undergoing treatment for hepatitis C infection need to see their doctors often. They need frequent blood tests to show if the liver is improving and whether or not the virus has fallen to undetectable levels. There are three categories of people in treatment: responders, nonresponders, and relapsers. Responders have a sustained response to treatment, meaning that their liver tests show improvement. The level of virus in their blood falls so low that it cannot be detected. Someone is a nonresponder if liver tests show little or no improvement and if the virus continues to be detected in the blood.

Some responders are unlikely to have a relapse, or a return of active infection, for as long as fifteen years after treatment. Other people who initially responded to treatment relapse within a few months. Liver enzymes become elevated once more, and the virus is again detected in the blood tests of these relapsers. Some patients may benefit from additional treatment. Doctors are considering the possibility of leaving certain patients on ribavirin and peginterferon for an indefinite number of years if they can tolerate the medications.

*When Charlie finished his peginterferon treatment, he felt it was worth all the side effects. He says, "My doctor told me the virus was at undetectable levels, that it had all but disappeared from my body. I've regained most of the weight I lost. My energy is coming back, and I'm working nearly full time again. It's really nice to be back in the classroom." Unfortunately, after six months, the virus level in Charlie's blood was high once again. His doctor said that he was a relapser and that more treatment might be needed. Charlie said he could not tolerate more treatment right away. "There's a lot of research going on," he said, "and maybe some of the new medications will be easier for me to take."*

## LIVER TRANSPLANT

Chronic hepatitis C is the most common reason for liver transplants in the United States. Each year, between eight thousand and ten thousand Americans who cannot get transplants die of liver disease caused by hepatitis C infection. Health authorities estimate that because so many people have chronic hepatitis C (an estimated 3.2 million Americans), the number of deaths may double or even triple over the next twenty years. Many of these people could be saved with liver transplants.

Some people with hepatitis C infection are not medically eligible for a transplant because they are too ill or have other health conditions that make a successful liver transplant unlikely. Of the thousands of people with hepatitis C infection who are medically eligible for liver transplants, only about a thousand receive new livers each year. Most people who qualify for transplants cannot receive one because of the shortage of available livers. According to the United Network for Organ Sharing, the organization responsible for coordinating organ transplants in the United States, nearly sixteen thousand people are on the waiting list for new livers. In total, approximately six thousand livers are transplanted each year for all medical conditions. Kidneys are the only organs that are more in demand than livers.

When a patient receives a liver transplant without having taken the peginterferon-ribavirin treatment first, the new liver nearly always become infected with hepatitis C. Even people who received the treatment may experience a recurrence of infection because small amounts of the virus often remain in the blood or bone marrow. After organ transplant, patients receive antirejection medications to decrease the risk of rejection. However, these medications also increase the chance of recurrent infection with hepatitis C (and other viruses and bacteria) because they slow down the body's immune system.

Doctors recommend that some patients with hepatitis C infection continue to take peginterferon and ribavirin after a liver transplant. Even with treatment, it is not unusual for patients infected with the hepatitis C virus to develop inflammation and damage to their new livers within a few years of transplant.

# CHAPTER SIX

# LIVING WITH HEPATITIS

Jackson hardly ever thinks about his past. The troubled teen who stole to support his heroin habit is just a bad memory. Jackson works hard at his job and just received a promotion. When the local blood bank came to Jackson's office for a blood drive, he was first in line to donate. But the nurse screened a sample of his blood before the donation process. She told Jackson that he could not donate blood because he had failed the screening. She said he might have hepatitis and he should see his doctor right away. Jackson always knew that intravenous drug use could lead to hepatitis C. But he'd never gotten sick back in the days when he was shooting up, so he thought he was safe.

Some patients with viral hepatitis never experience any discomfort or symptoms related to their disease. However, many others suffer significant problems that interfere with daily activities such as going to work, attending school, keeping up with family responsibilities, and staying in touch with friends. The symptoms of hepatitis can greatly affect the overall quality of life. People may become depressed and lose interest in the things that used to make them happy. Their physical symptoms can keep them from doing normal everyday things, such as shopping, preparing meals, and even maintaining personal hygiene.

Patients with acute hepatitis (A, B, or C) will feel sick for only a few weeks or months. Patients with chronic hepatitis B or C may experience symptoms for many months, perhaps even off and on for years. The problems and symptoms will be similar, regardless of which form of viral hepatitis a person has. What differs is the severity of the symptoms and how long they last.

People undergoing long-term treatment with antiviral medications and peginterferon may face additional problems related to side effects of their medications. People who receive liver transplants must take additional medications for the rest of their lives. Those medications can also cause side effects and complications. In spite of these problems, most people with hepatitis continue to carry on normal, active lives, whether or not they are undergoing treatment. Everyone can take positive steps to maintain the best possible health and to feel better.

## Managing Symptoms

### FATIGUE

Many people with hepatitis say what bothers them the most is the constant severe fatigue. Doing small everyday things can be difficult. Not only is the battle between the hepatitis infection and the immune system exhausting, but the liver disease can cause other parts of the body to work improperly. Even so, people should not assume their fatigue is due to the liver disease. Fatigue can result from any of the following:

- Heart disease
- Kidney disease
- Thyroid disease
- Anemia (low red blood cell count)
- Nutritional problems, such as low levels of iron, protein, or sodium
- Depression
- Side effects of medications
- Too much caffeine or alcohol
- Lack of exercise
- Insomnia (not enough sleep)

People with hepatitis need to learn to manage what energy they have. For example, many people feel better in the morning. They have less fatigue earlier in the day and more in the afternoon. Morning might be the best time to go shopping, exercise, keep medical and dental appointments, and visit friends. It is best to spread activities out over the course of a day or even several days. In other words, a person with fatigue related to hepatitis probably will not want to visit the doctor and go grocery shopping on the same morning. Instead, it might be better to plan the week's activities to conserve energy.

For some people, fatigue comes on suddenly. They must stop what they are doing and rest. Many people with hepatitis learn to make time for an afternoon nap. Even a nap of only thirty minutes can be a big energy booster. Busy people who have never napped during the daytime may be surprised to discover how much better they feel when they are rested.

People who feel well enough to keep working can bring a note from their doctor asking the employer to provide the time and a comfortable place for a short afternoon nap. Depending on the size of the company, labor laws require employers to make reasonable accommodations for disabled or sick employees. Smaller companies may not be bound by these laws.

## INSOMNIA

Most of us have trouble sleeping now and then. This is true of people with hepatitis as well. They can do several things to help themselves sleep better at night. They should never use alcohol, herbal remedies, over-the-counter medications, or nutritional supplements to help themselves sleep without their doctors' knowledge and permission. Some prescription medications may help insomnia, but a doctor will prescribe those with care in people with hepatitis. Not only might the medications interact badly with other medications the patient is taking, but they may make the recovering liver's job even more difficult.

Some commonsense measures that can improve sleep for people with or without hepatitis include the following:

- Establish a regular time to go to bed and to wake up.
- Make sure the bedroom is dark and quiet.
- Make the room a comfortable temperature; cooler may be better.
- Avoid eating or exercising several hours prior to bedtime.
- Avoid drinking coffee, cola, and other caffeinated beverages after lunch.
- Allow time in the evening to unwind before going to bed.
- Use the bedroom only for sleep. Don't eat or watch TV in bed.
- If you do not fall asleep within thirty minutes, get out of bed and do another activity until you are sleepy.

## DEPRESSION AND ANXIETY

People with hepatitis may become depressed. The medications used to treat hepatitis can cause depression and other psychological symptoms. Interferon has been linked to depression, irritability, confusion, insomnia, and difficulty concentrating. Also, it is common for people with nearly any chronic medical condition to become depressed. After all, people may not be able to do the things they normally do for fun. Up to 30 percent of people with chronic hepatitis C suffer from depression.

No one should feel ashamed or be reluctant to talk to a health-care provider about depression. Being anxious or depressed can make an already sick person feel much worse. Talking to a trusted friend or family member about depression and anxiety helps a lot. In some cases, visiting a counselor or therapist can also help.

Evelyn McKnight deals daily with the physical and psychological impact of chronic hepatitis C. She discovered her outpatient cancer treatment center had reused needles and given hepatitis C to more than ninety people including her. She has set up a nonprofit organization to fight for proper procedures with needles and syringes.

People with hepatitis and those close to them can join a hepatitis support group. (See "Resources" on page 122 for help in locating a support group.) Hepatitis patients can learn a lot from one another about how to manage their condition and the physical and mental problems that may come with it. Meditation and guided imagery can help many people. Guided imagery is the process of using thoughts to focus and guide the imagination. It's based on the concept that the body and mind are connected. Using all the senses, the body responds as though what is imagined is real. For example, a person with hepatitis can visualize his or her body successfully killing off the viruses.

Sometimes, a doctor prescribes antidepressant or antianxiety medications for patients with hepatitis. Controlling depression or other psychological problems with such medications can be tricky. Most medications are processed by the liver, and a sick liver will only face additional challenges with more medications. Still, some patients and their physicians may feel the benefits outweigh the potential side effects. Each patient and his or her doctor must make the decision after considering all the pros and cons.

*Once Jackson got over the shock of finding out that he might have hepatitis, he followed the advice of the blood bank nurse and visited his family doctor. "For the past twenty years, I've felt really good and have lived a completely normal life. I don't have any symptoms of the infection. I guess my past drug use was bound to catch up with me someday," he says. His doctor ordered several sophisticated blood tests called viral studies. "These will tell us what we're dealing with," the doctor told him.*

## Maintaining a Healthy Diet

A diet is all the food and liquids the body takes in. Many people with hepatitis can have a near-normal diet, while others need to follow the recommendations their doctors may provide. In general, people with hepatitis, like everyone, do best when sticking to a diet that is healthy and nutritious. That includes eating well-balanced meals that are low in fat, sugar, and salt. Whole grain bread, cereal, and pasta, along with a wide assortment of fruits and vegetables, are part of a healthy diet.

People with hepatitis may have a decreased appetite or even nausea, especially if they are taking medications, such as interferon. Eating five to six small meals each day may be easier than eating the three big meals most of us are used to eating. Keep in mind that the liver is responsible for filtering and processing almost everything we eat and drink. A damaged or sick liver needs all the help it can get. While people with hepatitis should always talk to their doctors about their diets, the following guidelines apply to most people with liver infections:

- Avoid all alcohol. It is toxic to a liver infected with hepatitis.
- Drink eight to twelve glasses of water each day, unless a doctor says otherwise.
- Some people will need to limit their salt intake. This helps to decrease extra fluid in the body. Read food labels to find the unexpected sources of salt and sodium, such as in canned soups and vegetables and processed frozen foods.
- Avoid excess caffeine. Have no more than three cups of caffeine-containing drinks per day. Coffee, cola, so-called power drinks, cocoa, and chocolate milk all contain caffeine.
- Talk to a doctor about taking vitamins. People with liver infections may need to restrict vitamins A and B3 and to increase others.
- Do not take iron (including that found in most vitamin supplements) without the doctor's permission. Some people with liver disease may have excess iron stored in their livers. High levels of iron can be damaging.
- People with cirrhosis due to hepatitis may need to eat less protein. Too much protein can lead to a harmful buildup of ammonia in the body. This may cause encephalopathy.
- Go easy on foods with lots of sugar and fat, including candy and baked goods such as cakes, pies, and doughnuts. (This is a healthy step for everyone, not just for people with hepatitis.)
- Maintain a healthy weight. For some people with hepatitis, this could mean gaining weight.
- Avoid all dietary supplements and herbal remedies unless approved by the doctor.

People can visit nutritionists or dieticians to learn how to make better food choices. In most cases, a liver-healthy diet can be as satisfying as a normal diet. It's a matter of making the right choices and finding new favorites.

## Sticking to an Exercise Plan

Some people with hepatitis might ask why they should exercise when they already feel tired. In general, exercise helps people feel better and may even improve their response to medical treatments. There is no reason why most people with hepatitis should not be able to perform some kind of exercise. It is always a good idea for people to check with their doctors before beginning an exercise program. Exercise can have the following positive effects:

- Improves the state of well-being and creates a better self-image
- Increases energy and alertness
- Improves functioning of the heart and lungs
- Controls total body fat, allowing the liver to work more efficiently
- Adds lean muscle mass

It is not necessary to exercise to exhaustion. Thirty minutes of moderate exercise five to six days a week can help someone with hepatitis feel a lot better. If that person has more energy in the morning, then early morning might be the best time to exercise. It's a good idea to start out with five to ten minutes of exercise and build up time gradually. People don't have to buy expensive exercise equipment or join a gym to get exercise.

An exercise plan should include both aerobic and weight-bearing workouts. Aerobic exercise includes brisk walking, swimming, bicycling (either a regular bike or a stationary one), and using a

Exercise and healthy eating are important for everyone, but especially for those living with chronic illnesses such as hepatitis.

treadmill or similar equipment. Aerobic exercise strengthens the heart and lungs and helps the liver work better.

Weight-bearing exercise builds up bones and muscles. This helps people who might have lost strength and muscle mass due to poor appetite and the muscle wasting that sometimes comes with hepatitis. Weight-bearing exercise can be as simple as lifting free weights at home or as elaborate as going to a gym and working out with a trainer on weight machines.

## Liver Transplants

Between 13,000 and 15,000 Americans die of chronic hepatitis B or C each year. Health officials believe that the number of deaths is certain to increase over the next twenty years as people who are unknowingly infected with the virus become ill. About 240 people with hepatitis B receive liver transplants each year, while 1,000 people with hepatitis C receive transplants. By some estimates, the need for liver transplants will increase sixfold over the next decade. Thousands of people could benefit from liver transplants, but there is a chronic shortage of donated livers.

Many people, including an increasing number of teenagers, decide to become organ donors in the event of a deadly accident or an unexpected fatal illness. In most states, that information is printed on a person's driver's license, so that doctors and nurses know the wishes of a patient who is brought into an emergency room. Family members may find some comfort in knowing that their loved one saved the lives of others through the generous gift of organ donation.

**Organ/Tissue Donor Card**

**I wish to donate my organs and tissues. I wish to give:**

☐ any needed organs and tissues          ☐ only the following organs and tissues:

_____

Donor
Signature _____ Date _____

Witness _____

Witness _____

An organ donor card from the U.S. Health Resources and Services Administration

USA TODAY

www.usatoday.com

**Life**
SECTION D

**JANUARY 26, 2009**

From the Pages of USA TODAY

# Proposal: Sign a donor card, move up on transplant list

**Who gets organs as waiting time, needs increase?**

Amanda Hayes, 39, of Yazoo City, Miss., has been waiting for a kidney since 1994. She favors giving preference on the national organ donation list to recipients who have taken good care of their health, despite their disease, and who would take care of the new organ.

For people like Hayes, waiting is one of the most frustrating parts of needing a new organ. And more people are waiting in the USA than ever before. The national organ transplant waiting list tops one hundred thousand, according to the United Network for Organ Sharing (UNOS), the nonprofit organization assigned by the federal government to maintain the list. UNOS says 45% of patients on the list have been waiting two or more years for a kidney, heart, liver, or some other organ.

The growing list of Americans waiting for organs prompted David Undis, president of the non-profit organ donation network LifeSharers, to propose last fall that UNOS reorder the list to give preference to patients who had agreed to become organ donors before their illness. The waiting list is now calculated

The practice of living donor liver transplants is becoming more common. A healthy human liver can regenerate to its full size even when more than half of it is removed. If someone with hepatitis qualifies for a liver transplant, a family member, spouse, or even a friend may be able to donate part of his or her liver. Years ago, only three out of ten people who received liver transplants lived longer than one year. Currently, between 85 and 90 percent of liver recipients survive for at least one year and 75 to 85 percent live five or more years.

to give the sickest patients the highest priority.

Undis says only half of the people eligible to become organ donors actually sign up, meaning millions of viable organs are buried with their original owners every year. Creating "A" and "B" priority lists favoring those committed to becoming organ donors would greatly increase the number of people who sign up to be donors themselves. No one would want to take the chance of ending up on the "B" list, Undis says.

UNOS president Robert Higgins, a heart surgeon, concedes that there are problems with the list, starting with the fact that minorities are disproportionately represented. "Certain populations wait a long time. We need more organs."

UNOS processes 7,000 to 8,000 organ donations each year. And while organ transplantation, once a chancy procedure, has become more

routine, Higgins says the demand has increased as the U.S. population has aged and people have become less healthy.

—Chris Joyner

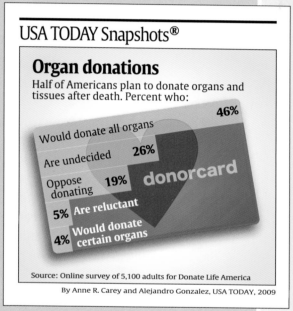

**USA TODAY Snapshots®**

**Organ donations**

Half of Americans plan to donate organs and tissues after death. Percent who:

46% Would donate all organs
26% Are undecided
19% Oppose donating
5% Are reluctant
4% Would donate certain organs

donorcard

Source: Online survey of 5,100 adults for Donate Life America

By Anne R. Carey and Alejandro Gonzalez, USA TODAY, 2009

People with liver transplants face a special set of challenges. Transplant patients must take powerful antirejection medications for the rest of their lives. These medications suppress the recipient's immune system, so the body does not reject the new liver. In the past, one out of five livers was rejected, even with medications. In the twenty-first century, that figure has dropped to about one out of fifty. People on antirejection medications are much more likely to come down with infections than are other people. They must do everything they can to avoid being exposed to someone who is sick with a cold, flu, or other infection. Still, a liver transplant greatly improves quality of life for many people. Most can return to their normal activities.

## Protecting Others

Most people with hepatitis do not want to infect others. It is important for them to inform all health-care providers (dentists as well as doctors) that they have hepatitis before any appointment. In addition, people should take necessary steps in their daily lives to protect others. Men who get shaves in a barbershop and women who get manicures and pedicures should tell those service workers about their hepatitis. People should cover open cuts or sores until they have healed.

Protecting others includes protecting the unborn. Women with hepatitis have a lot to consider if they want to become pregnant. A woman who is undergoing treatment with peginterferon, with or without other antiviral medications, should avoid pregnancy until she has completed the treatment because the medications can cause birth defects. However, if a woman's hepatitis is stable and her liver has not been badly damaged, she will usually deliver a healthy baby. Ideally, women with hepatitis should talk to their doctors before becoming pregnant.

*Jackson felt really lucky. The blood tests showed that while he was once infected with hepatitis C, he is now clear of active infection. Jackson is one of the fortunate people who recover from acute hepatitis C without any lasting liver damage. The doctor said Jackson probably recovered within six months of becoming infected. After Jackson and his wife discussed the results with the doctor, they decided she wouldn't need to be tested for hepatitis. Since Jackson recovered long before they were married, she has never been in danger of getting the virus from him.*

# Promising Research

Have you ever read about giant icebergs? We can see only the part that floats above the water. The largest part of the iceberg is underwater and out of sight. Hepatitis C is sort of like an iceberg. We know that at least 3.2 million Americans have hepatitis C. But the true number of people infected with the virus is probably much larger.

Hepatitis treatment is a very big business. In 2005 the cost for treatment of hepatitis C patients was estimated at more than $2 billion. As thousands more people become aware of their hepatitis, the cost for hepatitis treatment is expected to more than quadruple. By 2015 it will be between $8 billion and $9 billion! The following are some promising areas of research:

- Tests to more quickly identify which hepatitis virus someone has. This research is particularly important in the case of hepatitis C infections, which are caused by a number of different genotypes.
- Using stem cells to regenerate liver cells. Stem cells are undifferentiated cells that can develop into any type of body cell. This research is controversial, because the cells come from human embryos. The process destroys the embryo, which some people believe is killing a child. However, scientists are looking at other sources of stem cells, such as bone marrow and those found in the cord blood of newborns and the mother's placenta. As they discover new sources of stem cells, the controversy over embryonic stem cell research should decrease.
- Fresh or frozen liver cells used to regenerate healthy liver cells in those with hepatitis. This potentially decreases or postpones the need for a liver transplant.
- Development of an artificial liver for temporary use until a liver transplant becomes available
- Development of a super blood purifier that strains hepatitis C virus from the blood

June 8, 1999

www.usatoday.com
USA TODAY
Life
SECTION D

From the Pages of USA TODAY

# Millions hit hepatitis-C deadline: As silent killer roars, medical science struggles to find response

The hepatitis-C virus [HCV] probably has been inside Mary Johnson for 30 years. After the birth of her daughter, she had an emergency hysterectomy and received 7 pints of blood from strangers. That was in 1969, long before donated blood was screened for hepatitis C.

It takes decades for symptoms of disease to appear. Experts say the silent epidemic of the '70s and '80s, when the then-unrecognized virus was passed undetected through blood transfusions, is just beginning to show itself.

Blood transfusions before 1992 are thought to be the most common way hepatitis C has been spread. But a single injection of an illegal drug, a shared straw to snort cocaine, unprotected sex or a tattoo puts a person at risk.

Today's blood supply is considered safe, and the spread of HCV is waning, but the human price is yet to be paid.

- Work in genetics, the study of genes, to develop foods such as bananas and potatoes that contain the vaccine for hepatitis B. This could be especially important for poor countries without effective health-care systems. These countries often lack the trained health-care workers to administer the vaccines and the refrigeration needed to keep them fresh.
- A vaccine to prevent hepatitis C. Several potential vaccines are being tested.
- Researchers are working on new forms of interferon that have fewer side effects and shorter treatment schedules. New ways of

The liver, the body's blood filter, is known as the "silent organ" because it suffers silently with disease. Johnson says her liver "didn't talk to me. It never said, 'I have a headache.' " Now it must be replaced with a transplant if she is to survive. Johnson went to a liver specialist when her feet became swollen in 1995. Blood tests revealed HCV.

Johnson says it sometimes is a struggle deciding which treatments to try. Even waiting for a liver transplant makes her uneasy. More than half the patients who get new livers have the hepatitis-C virus return after the transplant.

"I am having some afterthoughts about having a transplant," she says. "A lot of the medications that you take afterward cause some debilitating effects. If I am to receive a liver, then it will happen. If not, I will go on with life as best I can. There are things in life you've got to accomplish, so you've got to go about your life and do those things."

There are thousands of women like Johnson. Studies have shown that during the 1970s and early '80s, 20% of the women who had Caesarean sections were given whole-blood transfusions either during the procedure or afterward to replace blood loss and speed recovery. A study in the mid-'80s found that up to 10% of surgical patients who received a transfusion developed hepatitis C after surgery. As many as 250,000 women contracted the virus that way.

Others at risk for the disease include anybody who received a blood transfusion or organ transplant before 1992. The Centers for Disease Control and Prevention says those people should be tested for the virus, along with anyone who has ever injected an illegal drug and health-care workers who have been exposed to blood on the job.

—*Robert Davis*

delivering interferon, such as intranasal sprays and time-release devices that can be implanted under the skin, are also in the works.

- New and better antiviral medications with fewer side effects to treat chronic hepatitis B and C. A dozen or more such medications are being tested in clinical trials.

Even though hepatitis can be a serious disease, it is manageable in most cases. Existing medications are a tremendous help, and those under development may have fewer side effects and may one day even offer a complete cure.

# Treatment: What Do You Think?

According to the National Institutes of Health, people who continue to use illegal intravenous drugs after being diagnosed with hepatitis can be treated with interferon and antiviral medications. But these treatments are very expensive, and many people lack insurance to pay for them. Government programs such as Medicaid, which is funded by taxes, pay the bills, which add up to thousands of dollars per treatment.

People with hepatitis might continue drinking alcohol even after their doctors tell them to stop. A liver transplant may cost half a million dollars or more. Also, patients must take expensive medications and have regular medical checkups for the rest of their lives. Some heavy drinkers find it difficult or impossible to stop drinking, even after a liver transplant. Drinking after a liver transplant puts the new liver in danger.

Some people believe health care should be based solely on medical need. Other people believe that destructive behaviors such as drinking and drug use must stop before they receive treatment. Should expensive medical treatments and hard-to-get liver transplants be reserved for people who agree to stop using drugs and drinking alcohol? Or should they be available to anyone who needs them? What do you think?

*Ethan recovered from hepatitis A without any treatment. Mai will probably have treatment for chronic hepatitis B after her baby is born. Jessica has just discovered she has hepatitis B and does not know if she will recover from it or not. Charlie has chronic hepatitis C and underwent a difficult course of treatment that ultimately failed to cure him. Jackson recovered years ago from an acute hepatitis C infection. Each of these people's lives and those of their families were touched by one of the viruses that cause hepatitis. An estimated five million Americans have viral hepatitis A, B, and C at any given time, making it a major public health problem. Fortunately, research on better ways to diagnose and treat all forms of viral hepatitis is under way.*

# GLOSSARY

**acute hepatitis:** a case of hepatitis that is gone in less than six months. Hepatitis A, B, and C can all lead to acute hepatitis.

**antibodies:** proteins produced in the body to help defend against invading foreign substances such as viruses and bacteria

**antiviral drugs:** medications used to fight infections caused by viruses, such as hepatitis

**ascites:** an accumulation of excess fluid in the abdomen, sometimes found in people with advanced hepatitis

**bilirubin:** a yellowish pigment released by red blood cells as they age and die. The liver collects and recycles bilirubin and excretes it as bile.

**chronic hepatitis:** a case of hepatitis that lasts six or more months. Hepatitis B and C commonly cause chronic hepatitis.

**cirrhosis:** severe scarring of the liver that can be caused by hepatitis (and other conditions). Cirrhosis is usually irreversible.

**contagious:** a disease that can be transmitted from one person to another. Colds and flu are highly contagious. All forms of viral hepatitis are contagious diseases.

**encephalopathy:** a state of mental confusion caused by severe liver damage (and other conditions) that may progress to death

**excrete:** to eliminate or discharge from the blood, cells, or bodily tissues. For example, people with hepatitis may excrete excess bile in the urine.

**fulminant hepatitis:** a severe form of acute hepatitis that results in permanent liver damage. It can be fatal if a liver transplant is not performed.

**genotype:** a genetically distinct variation of the hepatitis C virus

**hepatitis A:** a form of viral hepatitis, commonly passed via the oral-fecal route

**hepatitis B:** a form of viral hepatitis, commonly passed through sexual activity

**hepatitis C:** a form of viral hepatitis, commonly passed through contact with infected blood

**hepatitis D:** a form of hepatitis that occurs only in people infected with the hepatitis B virus

**hepatitis E:** a form of viral hepatitis that is passed via the oral-fecal route

**hepatitis G:** a form of viral hepatitis that is passed by blood and body fluids

**hepatocyte:** a single liver cell. Each hepatocyte can carry out most activities of the liver.

**immunoglobulin:** a medication prepared from human blood that contains concentrated antibodies. It can be used to help prevent hepatitis.

**incubation period:** the length of time between when a virus enters the body and the initial onset of symptoms

**interferons:** a group of proteins made by the body in response to viral infections. Synthetic versions are effective treatments for chronic hepatitis B and C.

**jaundice:** yellowish discoloration of the skin and whites of the eyes (sclera) that may occur in patients with hepatitis due to a buildup of bilirubin

**peginterferon:** a form of interferon that is injected once a week to treat chronic hepatitis B and C

**portal vein:** a vein that carries blood filled with nutrients from the intestines to the liver

**pruritus:** severe itching that can occur when the liver is damaged by hepatitis and other conditions

**toxins:** poisons; substances that can harm or destroy body cells and tissues

**vaccine:** a medication that stimulates the body's production of disease-fighting antibodies against a specific organism such as a hepatitis virus

**virus:** a tiny infectious particle that requires a living host (a plant or animal cell) to survive and replicate. A number of different viruses cause hepatitis.

# RESOURCES

### American Liver Foundation
**75 Maiden Lane · Suite 603 · New York, NY 10038**
**(800) 465-4837 or (888) 443-7872 · http://www.liverfoundation.org**

The American Liver Foundation (ALF) is the nation's leading nonprofit organization promoting liver health and disease prevention. ALF provides research, education, and advocacy for those affected by hepatitis and other liver-related diseases.

### Centers for Disease Control and Prevention
**1600 Clifton Road · Atlanta, GA 30333**
**(800) 311-3435 · http://www.cdc.gov**
**CDC's Viral Hepatitis website: http://www.cdc.gov/ncidod/diseases/hepatitis/index.htm**

The mission of the Centers for Disease Control and Prevention (CDC) is to promote health and quality of life by preventing and controlling disease, injury, and disability. The CDC conducts disease research to develop methods to better identify, control, and cure diseases. It also monitors and investigates health problems around the world and in the United States. It releases a *Morbidity and Mortality Weekly Report* (www.cdc.gov/mmwr), which tracks many health-related issues, disease outbreaks, and hepatitis case counts.

### Hepatitis B Foundation
**3805 Old Easton Road · Doylestown, PA 18902**
**(215) 489-4900 · http://www.hepb.org**

The Hepatitis B Foundation is the only national nonprofit organization solely dedicated to hepatitis B. Its mission is to find a cure and improve the quality of life for those affected by hepatitis B worldwide. The site offers extensive information in several languages about how to diagnose and treat hepatitis B, lists of liver specialists and support groups, and information about the latest research.

### Hepatitis Foundation International
**504 Blick Drive · Silver Spring, MD 20904-2901**
**(800) 891-0707 · http://www.hepfi.org**

This organization's mission is to educate the public, patients, and health-care professionals about the prevention, diagnosis, and treatment of viral hepatitis. The site has extensive information about new treatments and living with hepatitis and can assist people in finding a hepatitis support group in their area.

Hep-C ALERT
**660 NE 125th Street · North Miami, FL 33161**
**(877) 435-7443 · http://hep-c-alert.org**

This organization offers screening, information on support groups, and general education about hepatitis C, including a number of online informational videos in English and Spanish.

# SELECTED BIBLIOGRAPHY

American Liver Foundation. "Hepatitis A." ALF, November 27, 2007. http://www.liverfoundation.org/education/info/hepatitisa/ (October 20, 2009).

———. "Hepatitis B." ALF, September 28, 2007. http://www.liverfoundation.org/education/info/hepatitisb/ (October 20, 2009).

———. "Hepatitis C." ALF, October 24, 2007. http://www.liverfoundation.org/education/info/hepatitisc/ (October 20, 2009).

Centers for Disease Control and Prevention. "Epidemiology and Prevention of Vaccine-Preventable Diseases." 11th ed. CDC.gov. September 15, 2009. http://www.cdc.gov/vaccines/pubs/pinkbook/default.htm (October 20, 2009).

———. "Travelers' Health–Yellow Book." CDC.gov. July 27, 2009. http://wwwnc.cdc.gov/travel/contentYellowBook.aspx (October 20, 2009).

———. "2009 Child & Adolescent Immunization Schedules." CDC.gov. August 11, 2009. http://www.cdc.gov/vaccines/recs/schedules/child-schedule.htm (October 20, 2009).

———. "Viral Hepatitis: Statistics and Surveillance." CDC.gov. June 2, 2009. http://www.cdc.gov/hepatitis/Statistics.htm (October 20, 2009).

National Digestive Diseases Information Clearinghouse. "Chronic Hepatitis C: Current Disease Management." NIDDK, November 2006. http://digestive.niddk.nih.gov/ddiseases/pubs/chronichepc/ (October 20, 2009).

Stanford University. "A History of the Liver, Spleen, and Gallbladder." Early Science Lab. N.d. http://www.stanford.edu/class/history13/earlysciencelab/body/liverpages/livergallbladderspleen.html (October 20, 2009).

World Health Organization. "Hepatitis." WHO. N.d. http://www.who.int/csr/disease/hepatitis/en/index.html (October 20, 2009).

# FURTHER READING

Blumberg, Baruch S. *Hepatitis B: The Hunt for a Killer Virus*. Princeton, NJ: Princeton University Press, 2003.

Chopra, Sanjiv. *Dr. Sanjiv Chopra's Liver Book*. New York: Simon & Schuster, 2001.

Cohen, Mish R., Robert Gish, and Kalia Doner. *The Hepatitis C Help Book*. New York: St. Martin's Press, 2007.

Friedlander, Mark P., Jr., and Terry M. Phillips. *The Immune System: Your Body's Disease Fighting Army*. Minneapolis: Twenty-First Century Books, 1998.

Goldsmith, Connie. *Invisible Invaders: Dangerous Infectious Diseases*. Minneapolis: Twenty-First Century Books, 2006.

Horn, Lyle W. *Hepatitis*. New York: Chelsea House, 2005.

Murray, Patrick R., Ken S. Rosenthal, and Michael A. Pfaller. *Medical Microbiology*. 5th ed. Philadelphia: Elsevier, 2005.

Palmer, Melissa. *Dr. Melissa Palmer's Guide to Hepatitis and Liver Disease*. New York: Penguin Group, 2004.

Paul, Nina L., and Gina Pollichino. *Living with Hepatitis C for Dummies*. Hoboken, NJ: Wiley Publishing, 2005.

Sheen, Barbara. *Hepatitis*. Farmington Hills, MI: Lucent, 2003.

Worman, Howard. *The Liver Disorders and Hepatitis Sourcebook*. New York: McGraw-Hill, 2006.

Yancey, Diane. *STDs: What You Don't Know Can Hurt You*. Minneapolis: Twenty-First Century Books, 2002.

# WEBSITES

**MedlinePlus**
**http://www.medlineplus.gov**

MedlinePlus is an online service provided by the National Library of Medicine and the National Institutes of Health. It offers extensive health information on diseases and drugs, as well as the latest health news.

**TeensHealth**
**http://kidshealth.org/teen**

TeensHealth is a project of The Nemours Foundation, an organization established in 1936 by Alfred I. DuPont that is dedicated to improving the health and spirit of young people. Doctors and health care experts review all information before it is posted on the website.

# INDEX

## ABOUT THE AUTHOR

Connie Goldsmith is a registered nurse with a bachelor of science degree in nursing and a master of public administration degree in health care. She is the author of *Influenza, Invisible Invaders: Dangerous Infectious Diseases, Meningitis, Cutting-Edge Medicine, Superbugs Strike Back: When Antibiotics Fail*, and *Lost in Death Valley*. She has also published more than two hundred magazine articles, mostly on health topics for adults and children. She lives near Sacramento, California.

## PHOTO ACKNOWLEDGMENTS

The images in this book are used with the permission of: Centers for Disease Control and Prevention Public Health Image Library/Dr. Erskine Palmer, pp. 1, 3; © World History/Topham/The Image Works, p. 4; © Martin M. Rotker/Photo Researchers, Inc., pp. 5, 28; © Maksymenko 1/Alamy, p. 9; © Laura Westlund/Independent Picture Service, pp. 11, 58, 66; © Gladden Willis, M.D. /Visuals Unlimited, Inc., p. 13; © CNRI/ Photo Researchers, Inc., p. 15 (left); © Dennis Kunkel Microscopy, Inc./Visuals Unlimited, Inc., p. 15 (right); © Robert Nickelsberg/Getty Images, p. 22; © Arthur Glauberman/Photo Researchers, Inc., p. 25; © Dr P. Marazzi/Photo Researchers, Inc., p. 31; © Romilly Lockyer/The Image Bank/Getty Images, p. 34; © AJPhoto/Photo Researchers, Inc., p. 38; © Eileen Blass/USA TODAY, pp. 39, 77; © Medicimage/The Medical File/Peter Arnold, Inc., p. 42; © Alix/Photo Researchers, Inc., p. 43; © John Bavosi/ Photo Researchers, Inc., p. 44; © Hazel Appleton, Health Protection Agency Centre for Infections/Photo Researchers, Inc., p. 46; World Health Organization, pp. 47, 68; © Katye Martens/USA TODAY, p. 54; © Evan Eile/USA TODAY, p. 55; © BSIP/Photo Researchers, Inc., p. 60; © SuperStock/SuperStock, p. 62; © James King-Holmes/ Photo Researchers, Inc., p. 75; © Robert Hanashiro/USA TODAY, p. 80; © James Cavallini/Photo Researchers, Inc., p. 83; © Tek Image/Photo Researchers, Inc., p. 85; © iStockphoto.com/Paul Velgos, p. 86; © Olivier Voisin/Photo Researchers, Inc., p. 95; © Eric Francis/USA TODAY, p. 106; © Sean Gardner/USA TODAY, p. 110; Health Resources and Service Administration, p. 111.

Cover: © iStockphoto.com/Andrey Prokhorov (EKG); Centers for Disease Control and Prevention Public Health Image Library/Dr. Erskine Palmer (Hepatitis B micrograph).